Moments at Home

DEDICATION

To my parents, for not only teaching me how to create a stylish, welcoming and captivating home, but for also showing me how to inject every corner of every room with love.

STEVE CORDONY

Moments at Home

Interior Inspiration For Every Room

quadrille

CONTENTS

Introduction

I was once quoted as saying, 'styling is the simplest way to make a space "feel" a certain way … The space can be designed to within an inch of its life, but if there is no soul or representation of the people who live there then it becomes a showroom.'

This is still the mantra I live by, because in my mind the most interesting spaces to spend time in are the ones that constantly pique your curiosity. Spaces where there are myriad elements to look at – at once engaging and intriguing, personal and characterful – are what make a house feel like a home.

Today, working as an interior stylist for magazines such as *Belle* (to which I contribute as style director-at-large) as well as clients like Ralph Lauren, Wedgwood, French home fragrance house Trudon, Range Rover and Le Creuset, it seems inevitable I should end up obsessed with the interplay of the tiniest details that bring an interior to life. My Italian dad was a builder, my Maltese mum an interior decorator, and I was always around them, either building or renovating something, immersed in colour schemes, floor plans and building sites. I grew up on the North Shore of Sydney, in a heritage-listed house built in 1901. My love for entertaining comes down to these Italian-Maltese roots, where mum was always cooking, setting the table and styling the house with flowers and candles, while dad was keeping everyone entertained with outdoor games or projects.

Even in my teens, the idea of drawing the best out in a room was ever present. When mum and dad went out for the day, I would take all the furniture out of the lounge – the coffee tables, armchairs, lights, rugs, even the sofas – and I would start again, building up from the bare bones of the room, bringing things back in one by one to restyle the entire space. The funny thing is that even now, whenever I begin working on a new space or restyling a room, I take everything out (that's within my power to remove) and it's like a reset, where I start from a blank canvas and build the room up all over again in layers to create different moods.

I love mixing classical elements and giving them a contemporary spin. I never want a room to revolve around just one look or theme, I am always trying to mix things up so you can't pinpoint exactly the era or influence. In any space I reimagine, I try to add objects, furniture and accessories that complement one another – whether that's through colour, style or form – yet also contrast so that the space never feels one-dimensional.

At home, I combine different textures and finishes, mixing raw linen with velvet, gilt-framed mirrors with antique terracotta vessels, leather with jute, unpolished brass with honed marble, and ebonised furniture with faded antique rugs and time-worn urns. This encourages the eye to travel around a space, moving from one material to the next, appreciating the alchemy of raw and polished, light and shade, ancient and modern, rough and smooth.

My approach to styling a room is always instinctive. While my brain certainly doesn't work well with numbers, I can walk into any space and, as though I were wearing 3D goggles, know immediately where I would place the furniture and how I would draw it all together. I like imbuing rooms with a sense of scale and grandeur, and I value antiques because they convey such a sense of drama and history with their patina of wear. It seems ironic to me that when I was a teen, I would begrudgingly trudge behind my mum as she dragged me around antique shops at weekends, because now all I do in my spare time is scour markets and websites like 1stDibs in search of just the right thing.

I love the detailing of an ornate mirror that sits on a mantel or the carved crest of an armoire, but then I will pare these back by pitching them against an almost brutally stark white wall and an extremely minimalist contemporary light. My style lies in this constant tension between scale and proportion, and mixing textures and materials against natural, neutral backdrops so that it never feels like there is too much going on in a scheme. I want people to be instantly hit with the emotion of a room before they are able to start unpicking and peeling back its layers.

Despite being surrounded by these ideas of home décor all my life, I didn't grow up considering interior design as a career. When I was younger, I studied a lot of drama and music, earning a scholarship to The McDonald College of Performing Arts in Sydney. I later started a degree in industrial design at the University of New South Wales (UNSW), but only lasted six months because it was too maths-heavy and I knew my interest wasn't in the design of the product itself, but more about how it worked within a space and made someone feel. So I took six months off, working at my sister Amanda's deli (she's now food editor at *Australian House & Garden* and a caterer, specialising in wholesome home cooking), before enrolling in a one-year design fundamentals course at the Design Centre Enmore, home to some of Australia's best-known design courses. It covered multi-disciplinary modules of interior, graphic, jewellery, product and fashion design, and I loved the mix of all those creative genres working together; it's a frame of mind I still try to access in my work as an interior stylist today.

I moved on to studying interior design for another three years. For my final year project I was tasked with reimagining the Carriageworks, a multi-arts urban cultural precinct in Sydney's inner southern suburb of Redfern, and recognition for this led to me being awarded runner-up in *Belle* magazine's prestigious Young Interior Designer of the Year Award and an internship at the magazine. This is where I fell in love with the fast pace of creating whole worlds within a 6 m x 6 m space in just a few hours, before tearing it all down, putting it to one side and starting afresh again.

I stayed at the magazine for over five years before striking out on my own in 2014. I learnt how to style different homes for interior designers on photoshoots, where I would still pull everything out of the cupboards and the bookshelves to create a clean slate and then bring in truckloads of furniture to make it look cohesive and special. This proved to be an invaluable experience because I was finding out how interior designers put things together in terms of their own style and theme, and discovered how to add my own spin while staying true to their ethos and vision.

I love to have a mood board and a clear plan in place before starting any project. That way everything tends to run smoothly so I don't have to go back and forth, redoing things. Maybe it's how my brain works, but I need that sense of clarity and solid foundation from the beginning; it gives me the confidence to feel my way through the journey with assurance that the end result will be a success.

All of this has stood me in great stead for renovating various properties over the last two decades. I learnt very quickly that remodelling a home from scratch is a challenging process. It might be easy for me to walk into someone else's space and make changes, but when it came to Rosedale, (the 1887 six-bedroom house I breathed new life into with Michael Booth – a former marketing executive turned horticulturalist – on a 120-acre farm near Orange in the central tablelands of New South Wales) every decision became weighty and significant.

It wasn't just about visual aesthetics. It was about timings and budgets, ensuring everything aligned, and staying true to the farmstead's late 19th-century heritage while introducing contemporary touches. Michael has transformed the grounds into a sight of magnificent beauty, including the addition of a vast dam, Italianate pool, several converted outhouses and a nine-hectare paddock with 9,000 native trees and plants, as well as an abundant half-hectare vegetable garden at the back of the property. Over 30,000 shrubs, plants and trees have also been planted, including the propagation and cultivation of a selection of English, Japanese and Korean *Buxus* topiary.

A few sheep, a small herd of Belted Galloway cattle and two Shire horses, also share the property, as well as chickens, ducks, geese, doves, guinea fowl, white peacocks, a camel and two ostriches, Tanaka and Mariah (who had to be raised on a Bondi balcony until spring arrived in Orange). Two English springer spaniels, Bedford and new pup Wrenn, keep them all in check.

Surrounded by so much nature, it's no surprise that it informs my colour palette, and to a degree my textural choices. I never want my interiors to be just one note — one material, one finish, one surface. I like to work in a monochromatic way, using neutrals such as black, white, grey and ecru, but there's always one pull-out colour within every space, usually a bit dirtier in tone. For example, I love shades of green to dance around a room: as a highlight in a patterned fabric, the spine of a book, a glazed Chinese vessel, a plush velvet cushion and foliage in a vase. It instils calmness within a space. There are designers who deal so confidently with bold colour and vivid pattern, like Australian architects Arent&Pyke or British hotelier and interior designer Kit Kemp, but for me there's a simplicity and formality to be found working with a palette derived from one base tone that makes a space sing.

'I am going to make everything around me beautiful — that will be my life': this is one of my favourite quotes by the legendary early 20th-century American interior designer Elsie de Wolfe. It might seem a little shallow, but how our homes function and how we feel about ourselves when we are in them has a fundamental impact on our physical health as well as our mental wellbeing. Throughout every chapter of this book, I have tried to weave useful as well as inspirational ideas about how you can introduce effortless, uplifting moments of joy into every room: from touches of style that give you a little thrill every time you walk by, to arranging furniture, textiles and accessories in a way that entices the very best from each piece as well as the collective whole.

Each chapter highlights a different space in the flow through your home, starting right from the moment you or a guest approach the front door. I believe that every nook and niche of a room should be celebrated, even those that are often overlooked, such as a hallway or landing. From the entrance hall through to the living, entertaining and dining areas, to the kitchen and study, bedrooms and bathrooms, and finally the garden, I provide ideas on how to inject any space with some smart, considered styling to create a narrative that harmoniously threads throughout the house.

In the living room, I reflect on how this most public space in the home is a showcase for the cumulative memories of who you are and where you've been, while the dining room is somewhere I suggest you can be a little more theatrical and have fun with elements that instantly kick-start conversations long before the first course is served. In the kitchen, one of my favourite rooms in the house, practicality is of course key, but it is also about forging a space that is not only nourishing and nurturing for the body but also for the eyes and spirit.

Bedrooms are the most intimate of spaces, somewhere to seek comfort and calm, so I examine how to infuse softness and sensuality into rooms dedicated primarily to sleeping, looking at how they can encourage relaxation and rejuvenation as well. In the same way, a bathroom extends that feeling of being a place to seek quiet solace, so I discuss the many things you can do to make it somewhere you can take time to be kind to yourself. Drawing the shades and textures of nature into every space is always at the heart of my creative process, so naturally the garden is one of my favourite areas to style and spend time in. From creating a place to enjoy languorous alfresco lunches to setting up a little spot for afternoon tea or reading a book, there is so much you can do to extend the look and feel of your interior style into an outside space, whether that's a tiny terrace or a generous garden with gazebo, pool and sweeping lawn.

Styling, in essence, is the cherry on the top of what makes a room unique and memorable. It is

'If my LIFE'S PURPOSE *is helping people to* TRANSFORM THEIR HOMES *into* LITTLE WORLDS *that reflect their personalities …* I'M HAPPY *with that.'*

the editing of all those key elements – curating the special pieces of furniture, the objects found on your travels, the accessories that lend personality and charm – that ensures your attention within a room remains rapt. If my life's purpose is helping people to transform their homes into little worlds that reflect their personalities and resonate with all the journeys they have been on in life, then I'm happy with that. I'm never going to be a brain surgeon, but making things pretty – that I can do.

I love bringing people into my world, sharing with them the thought processes behind the whys and hows of my style DNA, whether that is creating a new vignette at home in Rosedale (probably too regular an occurrence, I'm not someone who is good at sitting still), hosting a Steve Cordony Masterclass in the garden or styling a shoot for one of the many brands I am lucky to work with. No one day is ever the same, which is both exhausting and thrilling, but I wouldn't want it any other way. Most importantly, whether it is through my Instagram feed (or whatever platform is invented in the future) or in the pages of this book, what I hope people will truly understand is the essence of what I strive to achieve in any interior – creating an intangible, metaphysical and captivating emotion that you can't quite put your finger on but in which lies the true magic of any distinctly personal, inviting and unforgettable space.

I

Welcome

Welcoming someone into your home starts long before they walk through the front door. The look and feel of the approach to your house sets the tone for what lies beyond, and it is as important to how you welcome guests to your home as it is to your own frame of mind. It's the last thing you see as you leave and the first thing you see when you return, so it needs to feel calm and collected but also inspiring.

Styling the front door with well-considered elements breaks that very hard line between indoors and out. I like to team an immaculately painted door with hardware in metallic accents, such as brass. I like a solid door handle and door knocker that feel good to the touch as well as kickplates, which are not only practical but also lend a little contrasting reflection and shine. At Rosedale, I am always changing up the plants around the front door – sometimes it is as simple as a standard bay, rose or olive tree either side of the door, or groups of pots filled with fresh herbs like rosemary, thyme, sage and mint, or citrus trees. For an element of drama, it could be pots planted with something sculptural (a swirly or ball-shaped box topiary, for example); or something loose and wild like potted feathery ferns or spiky dwarf date palms.

Equally, in the same way that a tablescape sets the mood for a dinner or party, styling the everyday look of your front door can be a fun way to ring the changes, seasonally or occasionally, marking Christmas or Easter, celebrating the arrival of spring or the abundance of autumn, or a special event such as a birthday or anniversary. It's almost like an amuse-bouche, in this case tantalising the eyes rather than the tastebuds, teasing out a sense of expectation of the style and personality that might lie within, as well as the promise of a memorable time for anyone spending time in your home.

Once inside, I like the entrance to feel light and airy because it eases you or a visitor into that very first instance of entering the home without feeling too overwhelmed. Whereas a powder room or dining room can be more theatrical, in an entry hall I like to keep the walls and architectural details light, airy and crisp. Set against this, I add in personal elements that will start to tell a story of what the journey will be like going beyond that initial welcome.

If there is space, a great console table, graphic rug and a moody artwork can really set the tone. You can even style it to feel like a room in itself – a long covered walkway to the front door can become a place to sit and take in the surroundings for five minutes; or you can create something akin to a foyer. In a house I styled in the harbourside suburb of Mosman, there was a space that served as the first port of call before you ventured downstairs into the kitchen and living rooms. So I introduced some chic armchairs, a coffee table and big pots of greenery to ensure it wasn't a wasted space that was used only as a thoroughfare.

If space is limited, which is often the case with entry hallways, a pendant or wall light can still make a bold statement. Probably my favourite way to introduce sculpture within a space is through lighting. I don't think lights need necessarily only be practical in the sense of providing light, I think of them as sculptural forms. I often bring in a generous mirror, which not only reflects the light around the space but also creates a sense of openness.

There is also a functionality to the hallway space, helping define where you place your keys and sunglasses when you walk through the front door; perhaps it is a tray or trinket box on the seat of a chair, or a console table with slim drawers where everything can go. A well-thought-out and well-designed hallway space should be both welcoming and practical.

Pattern unifies this hallway through the texture of the artwork by David Serisier on the wall, the glaze of the incredible twisted vase from Tamsin Johnson on the marble plinth and the rough woven wool and jute rug on the floor. Flowers are always my finishing flourish when I style a space, but they are also a must when styling the entrance of a home because they help to create a welcome on arrival as well as connecting the interior with the exterior.
/
Opposite: The entry to Rosedale teases all the elements you'll see as you move further into the home, including brass lanterns, antique rugs, greenery and European-style panelling. Contemporary art sits against a crisp backdrop of Porter's Paints Popcorn white walls and a dark Aniseed black door.

My love for a plaster or marble bust will never cease. The history they conjure and the grandeur they emanate will always transport me to another time and place, and they bring soul to an entry space.
/
Opposite: My favourite surface to style is a console table. With only a few elements, I love to tell a story that showcases my journey and personality. Here, on top of a vintage Italian 1960s console, I've displayed a bonsai tree to reflect a love of Japan; a contemporary Taccia table lamp originally designed by Achille and Pier Giacomo Castiglioni for Flos in the 1960s, which I coveted while studying interior design and was one of the first pieces I purchased when I started 'to make it' in the industry; and a bowl from a trip to India. The painting, a gift from the artist Kerry Armstrong, completes the scene.

This page and opposite: At a home designed by Alexander & Co., I styled an entry nook with antique Sicilian terracotta urns, handmade Japanese ceramics and stones found on a nearby beach to lend a patinaed contrast to the sleek grey polished-plaster wall.

'*I like to* KEEP THE WALLS *and architectural details* LIGHT, AIRY AND CRISP.'

This entry foyer in the country house is one of my favourite spots to reinvent on a seasonal basis. Using a framework of elements – table lamp, overscaled vase, stack of books and something fragrant (whether a diffuser, incense burner or candle) – I can switch each up according to the time of year or my mood to create a new aesthetic, whether on top of the antique chest of drawers or on top of an alternating plinth made in materials such as marble, wood or rattan.
/
Opposite: Sculptural foliage works not only to create a sense of drama and a strong focal point, but can be elevated on a narrow plinth to work in smaller spaces.

I bought 40 of these terracotta vessels from the side of the road in Scopello in Sicily. They have become a favourite accessory to style with as they are the perfect 'found' object to lend interest atop a console, mantelpiece or window ledge.

/

Opposite: A vintage rug from Cadrys 1952 proved the perfect addition to the entry hallway for this family home, designed by my friend Morgan Ferry, as it lends a sense of time-worn texture alongside the antique Chinese console, stacked ceramic lamp and contemporary box pendant lights.

In the entry passage of a Sydney beachside apartment, the mix of tan leather, scalloped timber, terracotta, travertine, brass and marble merges harmoniously. Styled for Mim Design.
/
Opposite: Playing with geometry helps to lead the eye in any direction you choose. Here, the vertical lines of the balustrade connect yet contrast with the horizontal lines of the upholstered Kelly Wearstler Fairfax Chair and the vertical lines of the Apparatus Studio pendant light. Styled for Arent&Pyke.

SUM UP YOUR STYLE I'm attracted to a clean and contemporary aesthetic which incorporates European detailing and contrasts both modern pieces and those that are storied with a past and patina.

LOW-LEVEL LIGHTING I buck the trend by using as few downlights as possible, preferring to focus more on task and mood lighting. And that's not only because the lights can act as an art form in themselves, adorning a room like a piece of jewellery; but also the mood they create is much softer and makes any space look better by providing little pockets of light that help direct the eye (rather than just having full-blown overheads, which starkly light everything). I use lights to help pinpoint specific moments, such as a beautiful table lamp on a console table that highlights the accessories you have chosen, or as a means of creating a glorious wash of light down a wall, illuminating the sculptural form of a chair against a honed stone or parquet wooden floor.

DESIRABLE DOORMATS Invest in a beautiful doormat: these days we're no longer restricted to the classic coir mat, there is a huge variety of outdoor rugs and mats to choose from that look and feel like the ones we use indoors (especially those made with recycled PET plastic bottles). Have fun exploring different colours or patterns that hint at the style of your home inside.

WELCOMING CHARM An interesting piece of carved or turned furniture, a dramatic chandelier or sculptural table lamp, a vintage rug or a decorative gilded mirror: these are the details that bring a more layered and textured ambience to an entry space but feel unique, each exuding its own sense of character and charm.

FABULOUS FOYERS In more generous spaces, create a foyer area with a round rug and a couple of armchairs to create an in-between space linking rooms such as a lounge and an informal dining room.

MINIMUM SPACE, MAXIMUM IMPACT A bust sitting on a little antique table with a round 18th-century portrait hung above, or the skinniest of consoles (just wide enough for a lamp, a bowl for keys and a scented candle) will work well in a small entry space. Or if there really is no room for a piece of furniture, create a gallery effect by hanging a series of framed photographs, abstract artworks or family portraits to bring energy to the space and introduce a flavour of the style you want to flow through the rest of the house.

SEDUCTIVE SCENTS I like to have a signature 'home' scent and then layer in complementary scents for different areas of the house. For the entry, I have Trudon's Ernesto, which is a deep, rich aroma with undertones of leather, tobacco, amber and moss.

POTTED PERFECTION At home there are a few varieties of plants on rotation, which I move in and out every month or so, including feathery Kentia palms, *Ficus lyrata* (fiddle-leaf fig) and olive trees. I love flowers or greenery in any space – scented or not – because they instantly bring a crisp freshness to the air.

A door pull and kickplate in brass provide an elegant finishing touch – acting almost like jewellery – to this front door.

II

Play

The Living Room

While the kitchen is at the heart of the home – a space where people gather to cook and start to create memories – the living room is where we showcase those memories. It's a place where we surround ourselves with the things that remind us of friends and family (near and far), our worldly adventures, the precious pieces we've collected over time, and perhaps artworks, textiles and books that inspire a little wistful armchair daydreaming.

The living room is the most public space in the home in which to project your style DNA. It is where you can tell the story of who you are and what you love, ideally styled against a backdrop of materials and textures that you instantly want to touch; ceramic pots, for example, with a patina that will keep on developing, adding warmth and depth to the living space and keeping the eye entertained.

In the living room at Rosedale, I wanted to create a visual flow where the eye never rests on just one thing. I want it to traverse the armchairs and the round table stacked with books, move across to the console tucked into the corner alcove – dressed with vases filled with foliage and lamps, paintings and books – and then back to the mantelpiece with its dazzling gilded mirror, before travelling up to the streamlined cornicing and elegant ceiling rose and down again, following the line of the magnificent crystal-beaded chandelier in the centre of the room. There is always something to see, the room never feels static.

When I approach the design of any space, I first consider the existing architecture. I look at the texture and quality of the walls, cornicing and skirting boards, the timber or stone of the floor, and the room's access to natural light. I use these to guide the floor plan so I can understand the building blocks needed to move the room plan from a one-dimensional idea to a three-dimensional practical space. I next look at the 'hero' items of furniture (sofa, armchairs and coffee table), then the occasional pieces (side tables, lighting, consoles and ottomans), where I like to play with the idea of organic forms juxtaposed with more angular ones to bring a dynamic energy to the room. I use floor coverings or rugs to help subtly demarcate areas into 'zones', and then think about the objects, plants, artworks and sculptures that will help to create height, working to draw the eye upwards. All of this is what gives a room its soul.

When choosing a piece of furniture, I look for designs that will be conducive to how people live today. Even the most sophisticated living room, where the family spends a lot of their time, needs to have a sense of comfort as well as formality. At a house in the upmarket suburb of Dover Heights, I styled the main living space with a voluptuously rounded 1970s-inspired B&B Italia modular sofa with puffy seats and backrests, because I knew the family wouldn't have to be forever fluffing up the cushions in order to keep it looking good. Plus, its bounciness really invited slouchy, convivial human interaction, making it a fun and practical choice as well.

In any room, but particularly in living spaces, I aim for a balance between light and heavy, plain and patterned. While bulky items like sofas, armoires and armchairs help to ground the room, I make sure the other elements feel softer. In the living room at Rosedale there is a plinth supporting an organic sculpture tucked into a corner, both in powdery all-white, a feathery baby birch tree stretching up to the ceiling in a rustic pot, and a trio of vintage Italian coffee tables with spidery legs; all interact with the bountiful natural light filtering through the room all day. Even an armchair upholstered in black velvet can be lifted and feel brighter with a shimmering edge of metallic studs.

At an incredible house located on Sydney's North Shore, the Australian interior designers Arent&Pyke designed a new modernist concrete pavilion attached to the back of a traditional Federation-style house. The large living space opens out to gardens that feel tropical and lush, so we chose furniture and accessories that harmonised rather than competed with the view. I love the interplay of different shapes and effects: the roundness of a pair of vintage Franco Albini bamboo chairs, the simplicity of a streamlined sofa, the busyness of a burl wood coffee table and the elegance of an antique chair, its seat covered in an intricate tapestry of colourful flowers. They all work happily together, while each individual piece brings its own story.

In a house in the harbourside suburb of
Mosman, the combined kitchen, dining and
living space was generous and light-filled, but
I wanted it to feel connected and intimate.
The rug demarcates the living area from the
dining table and kitchen island, and the soft
irregularity of the Minotti sofa is juxtaposed
against the graphic linearity of the table
and the geometric patterning of the iron
balustrade, with the neutral yet textured
colour scheme pulling it all together so it
doesn't feel too cluttered.

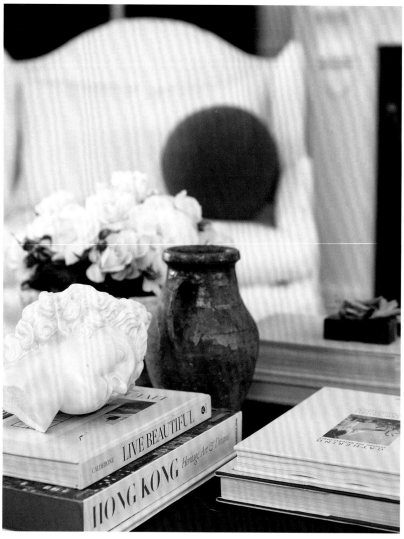

'I aim for a **BALANCE** *between*
light and heavy, **PLAIN** *and*
PATTERNED.'

The clean lines of the contemporary linen
sofa in this traditional-style living room make
it the perfect 'hero' item, around which I can
introduce and remove occasional pieces such
as a vintage 1960s Italian coffee table and
French rattan armchairs, contrasted with the
metallic side table and reading light, and the
abstract artwork by Robert Malherbe.
/
Opposite: The coffee table acts as the
room's central stage, where I am constantly
alternating layers of books, vessels, flowers
and quirky finds, sitting at different heights, to
inspire the eye to travel not only across the
table but also around the surrounding space.

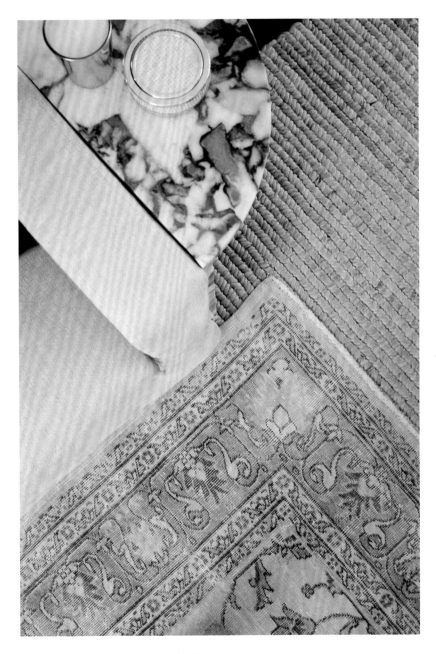

Rugs made with jute, sisal and abaca fibres
are among my favourite tools for helping to
define a space, especially when overlaid with
lighter vintage rugs, creating an interesting
and softening contrast.
/
Opposite: Patience is not my forte, but
I searched and searched for three years
before finding this perfect 18th-century gilt
and crystal chandelier, which delicately floats
above the mixed-era furniture in the living
room at Rosedale.

Colour used sparingly can make a big impact, especially if linking together certain objects around a room. In this beachside living space, the cushions in varying shades of blue velvet tie together the soft dusty hues of the coral, ceramic objects dotted along the shelves and the colour of the ocean outside the windows. Styled for Hugh-Jones Mackintosh.

This page and opposite: Whenever I style
a surface, I think about assembling clusters
of objects, but they should always be set
at different heights on different planes. I
create a low, mid and tall point when styling
a tabletop vignette. Here, fluttery *Scabiosa*
flowers bring height to a bulbous ceramic
vase, complemented by a bundle of tied
sage sitting in a low dish atop a stack of
books, which creates the midline, and then
a Dinosaur Designs resin dish brings the eye
down to focus on the beauty of the coffee
table's marble finish.

This page and opposite: Where space allows, an entrance foyer can also double as a cosy sitting room. Here, a pair of vintage swivel armchairs and a small settee, all upholstered in nubbly bouclé, team with a stone coffee table, a bentwood bar cart and sinuous Eileen Gray Roattino floor lamp to create a sense of arrival as well as a taste of the style of the rest of the home.

An apartment in the city fuses mid-century design with classical pieces. This was also my first foray into blending and balancing a variety of different eras and genres of furniture, lighting and accessories.
/
Opposite: The choice of colour palette powerfully dictates the mood of a space. In this living room of a suburban Sydney home, the hues of walnut and black lacquer for the chairs and commode feel rich and moody. Styled for Hugh-Jones Mackintosh.

I constantly strive to create the emotion of 'push and pull' across every surface. By contrasting highly polished elements – like a brass vase for blousy florals – with rustic handmade elements (a hand-wrought bust, a terracotta pot), I create depth even within a pared-back coffee table vignette.

This page and opposite: I'm not all about
neutrals. Touches of coral pink, smoky blue
and deep green dance peacefully around this
intimate living space, balanced by the hints of
brass, rattan, marble and dark shelving in the
room. Styled for Arent&Pyke.

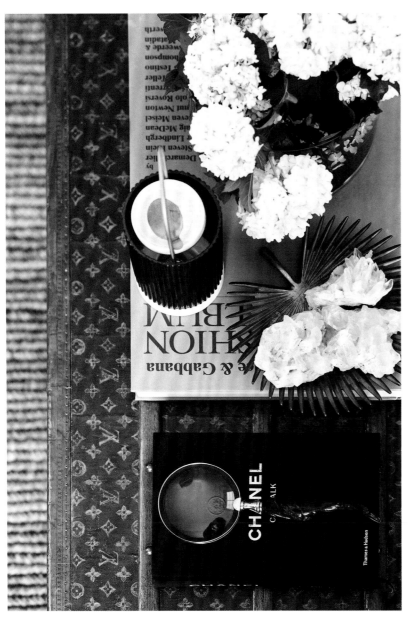

When styling any vignette, I look at every element from a different angle to make sure the heights, flow and rhythm of each object — and the 'moment' they create when grouped together — feel right, no matter from where the object is viewed.
/
Opposite: Creating a focal point in a room with an overscaled foliage installation has become one of my signature styling touches. It requires a heavy-based vase, two or three 'core' branches (to create a triangle) and a good pair of secateurs to shave each one down inch by inch until you find the perfect balancing point between each branch. Once you have the shape, you can also infill with an additional branch or two to flesh it out, or keep it sparse and striking.
/
Overleaf: The pared-back palette of this coastal apartment draws the outside in through the mix of natural textures, such as sandy bouclé and hand-knotted wool, worn wood, transparent glass and earthy ceramics. Styled for Mim Design.

This page and opposite: While working with
the incredible concrete proportions, checked
marble flooring and enticing garden vistas of
the modernist extension that Arent&Pyke
added to this old Federation home on Sydney's
North Shore, I was influenced by director Luca
Guadagnino's 2017 film, *Call Me by Your Name.*
Antique and vintage Italian furniture in a mix
of finishes, from burl wood and rattan
to needlepoint, and quirky modern lighting
were chosen to loosely represent characters
in the movie.

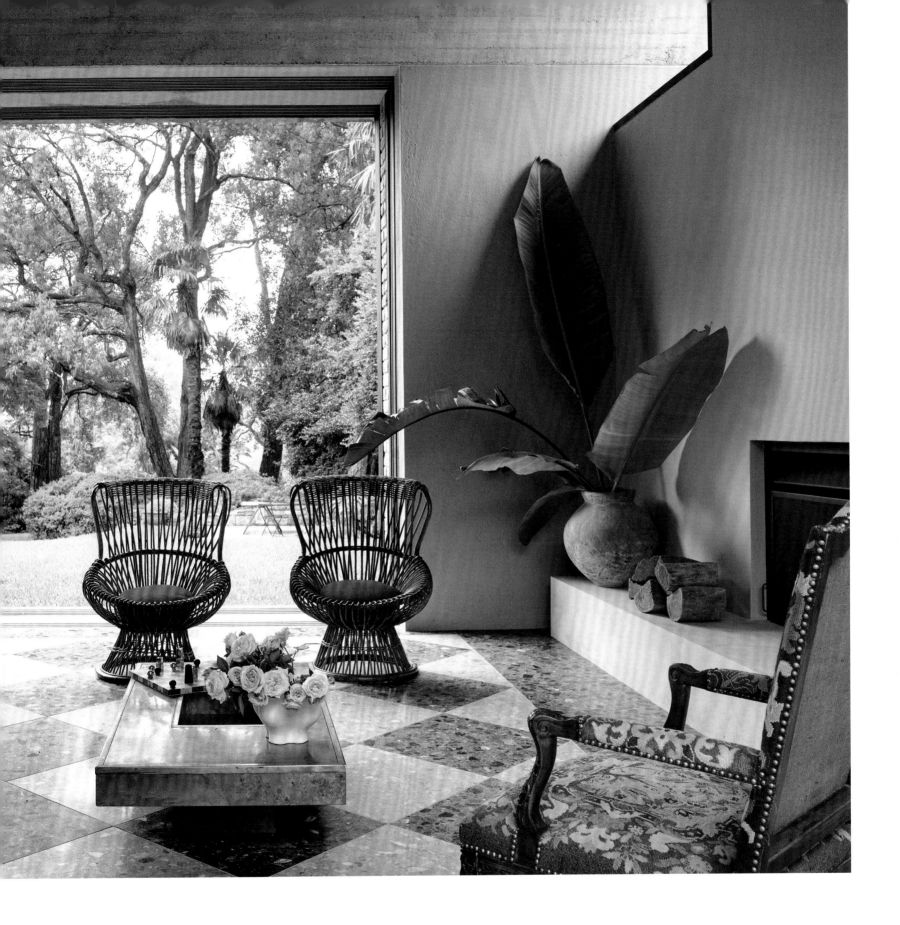

'The **TONAL PALETTE** *of this lounge room feels* **RICH** *and* **WEATHERED** *yet* **GRAPHIC**.'

This page and opposite: The tonal palette of this lounge room feels rich and weathered yet graphic. The marble fireplace, the ribbed detailing of the console and the sheepskin throw against the Halyard rope chair work in unison with the raised detailing of the rug and coffee table (topped with interesting pieces such as a Japanese ceramic vessel and gleaming recycled aluminium alloy dreidel and base by Tsu Lange Yor). Together, the effect lends a sculptural imprint to every surface.

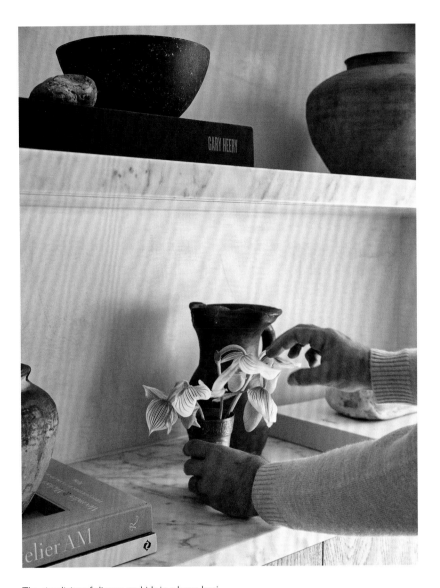

The simplicity of slipper orchids in a brass lassi
cup from India is sometimes all that's needed
to create impact on a shelf or tabletop.
/
Opposite: I love 'in between' spaces that
act like an entry foyer and also as a sitting
area. I had the pleasure of styling this space
for my dear friends Juliette Arent and Sarah
Jane Pyke, founders of Sydney-based design
practice Arent&Pyke, to link the front
door area to the main living space beyond.
Statement pieces, such as these Utrecht
armchairs by Gerrit Rietveld for Cassina, and
the Serge Mouille pendant light, don't need to
be restricted to the main living space. Here,
they create a welcoming moment in an area
that might otherwise have been left bare.

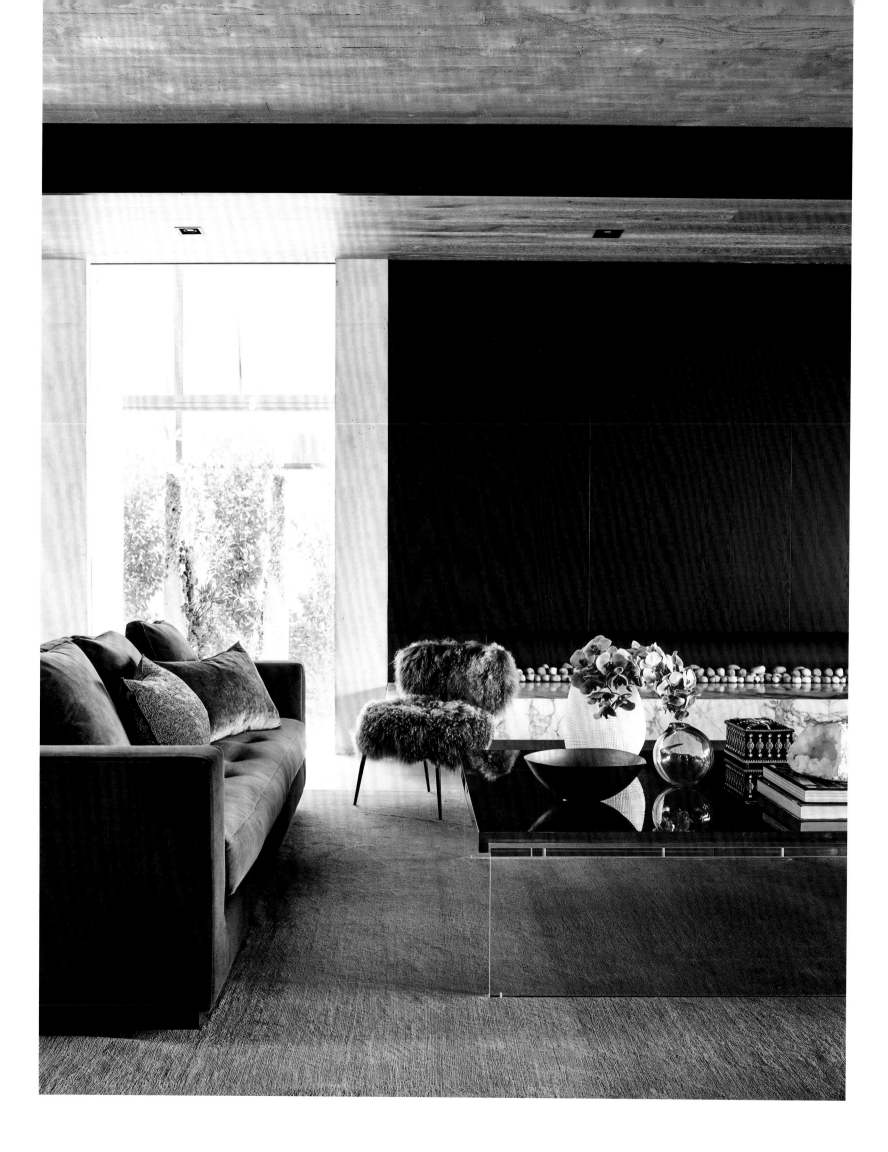

This page and opposite: The drama in this harbourside living room is amplified through the use of rich textures such as deep, dark velvet, cobalt sheepskin, amber glass, magenta orchids and quartz crystal all brought together by Darren Sylvester's hyperrealistic painting. Styled for Hugh-Jones Mackintosh.

SCULPTURAL SENSIBILITIES Within the mix of classic pieces of furniture, I love to throw in something sculptural and delicate – a mid-century brass wall hanging or light sconce, for example – that gives the eye a brief moment of textural respite from the heavier elements in the room such as armchairs and sofas. It lends a lightness or unexpected reverberation that keeps you curious. I don't like rooms that feel flat – there needs to be a lot of things for the eye to take in, but it shouldn't be styled so that you see it all at once.

MIXING CLASSIC AND CONTEMPORARY At Rosedale, I regularly top a drop-leaf walnut table with rustic urns and piles of books, which works in harmony with the abstract art on the walls and the pairs of high-backed armchairs, either upholstered in white with metallic studs or dark black velvet, which I swap in and out depending on my mood. The idea of weight and heaviness plays against delicacy and lightness, an ethos of complement and contrast I talk a lot about in my Masterclasses.

PLAYFUL PERSPECTIVES It would be easy to fill large wall spaces with oversized works of art, but I often choose smaller works that create specific focal points for the eye to be drawn towards and zoom into. It is less confronting and hectic. It also plays with proportion, and I find I'm sometimes much more drawn to an artwork that is smaller than I expect it to be.

MAP IT OUT Material-based mood boards can be useful in planning out a space, not only visually but also in terms of tactility. Gather together samples and start to layer them, beginning with the base and then building up the many different materials and textures that will form the interior blueprint of your space, whether it is one room or a whole house.

IN THE MOOD In a living room, creating an ambient atmosphere is key. Along with hanging one hero pendant light, I like to flank the sofa with table lamps and place sculptural floor lamps next to occasional chairs.

SOURCES
Becker Minty, Sydney and Hobart (beckerminty. com) for an eclectic, intriguing collection of designs for every room in the home from the best global brands.
Jardan, Sydney (jardansydney.com.au) for furniture, lighting and accessories made with sustainability and an identifiable Australian aesthetic in mind.
Boffi (boffi.com), for the ultimate in Italian contemporary design.
Cadrys 1952, Sydney and Melbourne (cadrys. com.au) for Australia's largest collection of collectible decorative and antique Persian, Anatolian, Caucasian and European rugs.
Tamsin Johnson, Sydney (tamsinjohnson.com) for an interior designer's tasteful curation of intriguing, eclectic, antique and contemporary furniture, lighting and accessories.
Restoration Hardware, US, UK, Europe and Canada (rh.com) for streamlined elegant contemporary pieces for every room in the home.
CC-Tapis, Milan and retailers worldwide (cc-tapis. com) for beautifully made, colourfully executed hand-knotted, crocheted or dhurrie woven rugs in collaboration with the world's leading designers.
Alex Eagle Studio, London (alexeagle.com) for a chic curation of home- and tableware sourced from artisans around the world.

VIVACIOUS VIGNETTES Creating an instant but enticing vignette is easy. My favourite combination includes a pile of coffee table books, a scented candle and a vase of flowers. Other things you can play with include ceramics, crystals, bookends, coasters and inlaid cigar or playing card boxes. Whatever you choose, always arrange them on different planes and at different heights (high, medium and low) to allow the eye to dance over each individual thing rather than reading it as a whole all at once. Create tension by pushing things back and bringing things forward – put a stack of books at the back of a console or mantelpiece and pull a vessel to the front of it rather than placing it by the side. A scented candle might be the low point in the arrangement, while a vase of flowers brings height. Constantly moving things around keeps arrangements feeling fresh. Remember to balance out raw and polished elements, team found objects with heirloom trinkets, and don't be afraid to add a whimsical addition alongside something sentimental. This will always give a well-lived, well-travelled feel to any vignette.

My favourite styling combination at Rosedale:
a mix of vintage Italian chairs, brass nesting
tables, contemporary sculptural ceramics, a
custom abaca rug and cushions embellished
with bird and floral motifs.

III

Nourish

The Kitchen

The kitchen, for me, is about nurturing and nourishment, not just because it is where I delight in cooking food for the ones I love, but also because these are the emotions that determine how I decorate and style the space. While functionality is at the core of a kitchen's design, it is just as important that it feels like a comfortable, convivial heart of the home, where people can gather and lively chats can unfold.

I go into a meditative state when I'm cooking, and there's something grounding and earthy about being on the land at Rosedale, where I can go out into the garden to forage for fresh produce for dinner. So when it came to designing and styling the kitchen on the farm, I purposely brought in the same visually nourishing colours, textures and materials that reflect nature's presence outside, because it is important to me that the kitchen feels as good as it functions well.

We spend a lot of time in our kitchens, so it makes such a difference to fill them with the things that keep us inspired and make our hearts happy. I bring in all the elements I would use in a bedroom, living room or hallway space. I have art on the shelves, whether resting against the wall on the bench or hung on a wall, and sculptures sit on the counter tops. I collect vessels that have great charisma, like the Chinese tofu pot in which I keep my utensils; I cover tops of stools in soft finishes such as smooth leather or slubby bouclé; and I fill huge turned wooden bowls with an abundance of ripe fruit, eggs or just-picked vegetables.

I love sourcing vintage chopping boards from places like Italy and Turkey because I've always delighted in how they were once used to present food. I'm drawn to intricate antique silver pieces like toast racks, egg cups and cake stands to lend a classical feel. And I love beautiful, handmade, utilitarian pieces that conjure basic notions of how the kitchen has functioned over the centuries — it might be an earthenware pitcher or a hand-painted platter that can be given a new lease of life, feeding into my love for the constant tension to be found in marrying old and new.

Bringing in greenery from the garden also adds an element of drama, as well as the opportunity to play with height. I use the branches that have been pruned back from trees and shrubs around the farm, so it's good for the environment and a wonderful way to bring the outside in. Or I might add something as effortless as a vase of graphic palm fronds — so simple, like big friendly waving hands — which, contrasting with a kitchen floor made of green checkerboard marble, instantly ties the space together in a verdantly light and relaxed way. It speaks to our very basic human desire to be as close to nature as possible.

The starting elements in this kitchen were the Ralph Lauren pendant (because I knew I wanted that punch of brass), the chevron reclaimed French oak floor and the Arabescato Vagli marble benchtop. Against this, I chose the restraint of Shaker-style kitchen cabinetry in a dark olive black and the same glint of brass for the tapware. Together these elements helped build the story of how I wanted the kitchen to feel — a little bit European meets Australian outback. I know the marble is going to mark, the floors are going to scratch and the brass is going to age over time, but I always lean towards using natural materials because tactililty often gets lost in very glossy, high-tech finishes. I like kitchens to feel alive, where personality can shine through.

A quirky, unexpected light hanging over a kitchen island or breakfast bar; a sofa for guests or kids to hang out on while you cook; books and handmade ceramics; stools with intricately turned legs; a delicate still life in a gilt frame: these are all elements that don't necessarily belong in a kitchen, but they all help to tell a story about how we live in a space that needn't be governed by rules around its historical use. Collections of utilitarian vessels can become their own form of visual art, so don't feel as though you have to hide everything behind cupboard doors. Having things out on display encourages you to use them every day. Even when I'm plating up a simple dinner, I'll choose handcrafted plates by Rina Menardi and Bitossi glassware. I feel like that's what the kitchen should be all about, everyday luxury, enjoying the tangible satisfaction of presenting lovingly prepared food in a place that brings everyone great joy.

Dominant materials like marble, rich timber and brass can be softened by objects imbued with a time-worn patina, such as old chopping boards, antique silver and pewter, and artful displays of delicious food, from fresh peaches to a homemade sponge cake. Styled for Arent&Pyke.
/
Opposite: When I style a kitchen, I swing between using everyday utilitarian objects and ornamental accessories that you would choose for any other space in the home. A gilt-framed artwork resting on a floating shelf mixed with handmade ceramics and a Murano glass vase might seem more apt in a lounge or bedroom, but by adding decorative pieces like these to a functional kitchen space it transforms it into something completely unexpected. Styled for Arent&Pyke.

I indulge my love for crescendos of overscaled greenery in the kitchen, where each month I play with different fallen foliage I've foraged from the garden: branches of oak, magnolia, dogwood, poplar, English elm or camellia. It creates a focal point that draws the eye upwards, making the standard height of our kitchen ceiling feel grander than it actually is.

The kitchen cabinets, painted in a deep charcoal green called Black Cockatoo by Porter's Paints, harmonise with the Arabescato Vagli marble benchtops, the classic Esse stove and the unlacquered brass detailing of the lighting, taps and joinery handles.
/
Opposite: In the mudroom-cum-laundry, a monochrome tumbled marble checkerboard floor is not only super-practical, but it is also a lively pattern that creates a continuation of the diagonal lines of the wooden chevron floorboards in the kitchen.

'I purposely brought in the VISUALLY NOURISHING *colours, textures and materials that reflect* NATURE'S PRESENCE *outside.*'

White on white works when there is enough texture in the objects and materials to stop the room from feeling one-dimensional. Veined Calacatta marble benchtops, a weathered timber cutting board, a stone fruit bowl, the turned wooden legs of the kitchen stools, and cherry blossom branches sprouting from an overscaled Korean moon jar bring an exciting energy to this corner of a kitchen in Mosman.

This farmhouse-style kitchen took its cue from Shaker-style joinery, painted in a deep blue-tinged charcoal hue, but contrasted with modernist lighting and quirky accessories to make it feel contemporary rather than traditional. Styled for Hugh-Jones Mackintosh.
/
Opposite: Functional but visually pleasing accessories can bring personality to a kitchen workspace. Here, an antique Chinese tofu pot holds cooking utensils, fresh farm eggs are nestled in a Japanese bowl (I always decant my eggs from the carton) and grainy chopping boards help to bring warmth to the otherwise utilitarian marble stovetop inset and splashback.

'*Collections of* UTILITARIAN VESSELS *can become their own form of* VISUAL ART.'

Tones of blue infuse the details of this harbourside kitchen, from the Gervasoni chairs and the scatter cushions to artwork by Jo Bertini, bringing the space a relaxed yet considered feel. Styled for Hugh-Jones Mackintosh.
/
Opposite: Just as I would style a vignette on a hallway console or coffee table, I do the same on a kitchen bench, grouping together utilitarian, yet sculptural, pieces such as hand-thrown ceramics, a sensuous marble oblong bowl and a stack of vintage Turkish chopping boards.

An open floating shelf in the kitchen is not only practical and accessible, but it also allows for character to be injected into a space, showcasing an evolving array of favourite kitchen and dinnerware pieces.
/
Opposite: I love a metallic accent for joinery, hardware and lighting, especially natural brass because it ages so well. Here, its warming patina brings a touch of sophistication to the guest house kitchen.

This page and page 84: This beachside kitchen designed by Alexander & Co. features many bold elements, including crazy-pave marble flooring and timber joinery which extends across the ceiling. I wanted to soften the overall effect by styling it with well-worn textures, from rough-hewn wooden accessories to rustic ceramics.

A mix of rounded silhouettes lends this kitchen corner nook a friendly cosiness, with the custom-made table's solid chubby legs and smooth elliptical top and the bulbous ceramic and glass vessels on top.

My styling 'rule of three' works perfectly in this kitchen vignette, where a stunning dogwood branch provides a high point next to the midpoint of the Jaime Hayon Réaction Poétique centrepiece and the stack of handmade plates as the low point. Styled for Arent&Pyke.

/

Opposite: Tones of teal, dark wood and brass lend a rich sophistication to this Melbourne kitchen by designer Morgan Ferry. While the workspace is streamlined, the accessories – including an Indian chapati box, vintage timber bowl and tall white handmade vase – elevate the room to feel embellished as well as functional.

I love to style and restyle, over and over again, this favourite nook in the kitchen at Rosedale. I'm always rearranging different elements, from the leaning artwork which helps to break up the back wall to a statement vessel, a low bowl for fruit, vegetables or eggs, and a vase of fresh flowers.

/

Opposite: My family is passionate about food, and when I am home, my favourite thing to do is spend time in the kitchen cooking, baking and, of course, styling (even the mixing bowls are tonal).

DRAMATIC OVERTURES I'm known for my striking arrangements of flowers and foliage. Always start with a heavy-bottomed vase and fill it with as much water as you can. Take three branches, between one and two metres long (depending on how dramatic you want to go), strip the leaves off the bottom and bash the ends until they're frayed, to absorb more water. Sit them in the vase in the shape of a triangle to form the supporting structure for your arrangement (if it starts to tip, take an inch off the branch on that side and if it tilts again, take another inch off to balance out the weight). Add more branches to the centre to fill out the arrangement. Go as high and wide as you dare, and as your vessel can support.

STYLISH COUNTER TOPS In the kitchen at Rosedale, I am always creating little vignettes on the kitchen counters. Page 88 depicts one of my all-time favourite moments, where the brass wall light talked to the colours of the Oriental print, bowl of eggs, vase of purple hydrangeas and striking cheetah vase.

Some of my favourite sources for kitchen and tableware include **Ginori 1735**, Milan (ginori1735.com) for iconic hand-painted Italian porcelain created in collaboration with leading designers since the 18th century; **The HUB General Store**, Melbourne (thehubgeneralstore.com.au) for utilitarian chic kitchen and homewares, from candles and soaps to pastry brushes and water jugs; **L'Objet**, Paris and New York (l-objet.com) for handcrafted tableware, home accessories, fragrance and sculptural pieces with an irreverent twist, including collaborations with Kelly Behun and the Haas Brothers.

PICK ONE PULL-OUT COLOUR Sometimes the very smallest detail makes the biggest impact. For example, upholster the tops of stools with leather in a bold shade of rusty red, marine blue or terracotta orange; or harmonise with the rich, warm shades that might stand out in a painting you might have propped against a backsplash or on a floating shelf with tonally hued coloured bowls or kitchen textiles. Emphasise the warmth of the wood lining the kitchen cupboards or countertop by adding in complementary accessories, such as large hand-carved bowls or grainy antique chopping boards. One pull-out colour will really stand out against the otherwise more neutral hues of white and grey usually deployed in a kitchen.

ACCESSORISE A KITCHEN LIKE A LIVING ROOM Don't be precious about how you accessorise a kitchen: hang an amazing artwork, such as a sculptural piece by the likes of one of my favourite artists, Tracey Deep; opt for interesting lights, like a contemporary bubble pendant light; fill open shelves with stacks of hand-thrown crockery. Bring in antique pieces – a decorative chair, a Victorian table as an extra work- or serving space, old wooden chopping boards dented with years of use – to add further warmth and interest.

STORAGE Clever internal joinery design is crucial to the overall functionality of a kitchen, but I also love sourcing non-traditional storage, like vintage baskets, vessels, pots or canisters to store utensils, spices, food or linen. It is so much more interesting to have things on show rather than tucked away out of sight.

DELICIOUS DISHES The colours of my go-to weekday dinner dish – baked ocean trout, steamed rice and sautéed leafy greens – pop all the more vibrantly when served on Jasper Conran for Wedgwood's 'White' day-to-day fine bone china. At the weekend, nothing beats pancake Sunday, and on lazy nights where only pizza or pasta will do, I opt for truffle mushroom.

IF IN DOUBT, START AGAIN Not everything goes to plan. If something doesn't feel right in a room, trust your instinct – it is important to pay attention to your emotional response to a space because it can make such a huge impact on the mood of a room and how you feel in it. Allowing yourself to sit with a space until the right layout, colour, wallpaper or design piece, such as a particular lamp or chair, presents itself is what I enjoy most about the creative process behind crafting an interior. The opportunity to embrace a little time out and some lateral thinking inevitably leads to a better floor plan or choice of colour or pattern palette.

SOURCES
Orient House, Sydney (orienthouse.com.au) for Asian and African furniture, porcelain, baskets, pots and planters, masks and lanterns. Also **Ondene**, Sydney (ondene.com.au) for striking, modern pieces by the likes of French designer Christophe Delcourt, Austrian crystal house Lobmeyr and Belgian designers Michaël Verheyden and Kerstens.
For classic kitchen hardware, I love **The English Tapware Company** (englishtapware.com.au) and **The Water Monopoly** (thewatermonopoly.com); for unique metalwork, **Anna Charlesworth** (annacharlesworth.com.au); and **McMullin & Co.** (mcmullinandco.com) for a modernist curation of contemporary furniture, lighting, art and accessories.

Here a large Korean Moon jar and Indonesian reclaimed trivet lend depth, interest and boldness in shape to what is otherwise a pared back French-inspired kitchen.

IV

Celebrate

If the living room is the heart of a home, and the kitchen is like its belly, then the dining room embodies its celebratory spirit. This is a space that brings people together in conversation and laughter, gathering them in a great big hug. A dining room should be fun, joyful and genial, whether you're throwing a grand, glamorous soirée or a tiny gathering with just a couple of friends and a takeaway. No matter its size, the dining room is a place to introduce a touch of theatrics and playfulness, to bring out tantalising details that will get the conversation started long before people have even sat down to dinner.

Dining rooms are like powder rooms, where you can afford to be a little braver, bolder and quirkier to create an atmosphere that is immediately transporting and convivial. In the dining room at Rosedale, I lined the walls with a dramatic 19th-century-inspired wallpaper by Iksel, a fantastical reinterpretation of a centuries-old tapestry that wraps around the room in 360 degrees, completely enveloping the space. It was something I'd had stored away in my folder of thousands of inspirational pictures, years before renovating the farm, and I knew it would work perfectly here. It speaks to the mix of old and new that I'm always drawn to, and its muted colour palette works almost like a neutral, with the white chair rail at the bottom allowing it some breathing space. The landscape of mountains and monkeys playing in the palm trees makes it fun to experience and explore.

A good starting point for this room is the dining table, as the hue and texture of its materiality and its silhouette – whether traditional or contemporary – will help to set the tone for the rest of the space and influence whatever else you layer with it. At a house in Dover Heights, Sydney, a sculptural table with ridged supports makes a dramatic contrast with the hard lines of the black-steel-framed dining chairs. In a Darlinghurst apartment, the curvaceous mix of Thonet bentwood café and Carver chairs complements the rounded Saarinen table; at Garden House, the clean lines of cantilever tubular chairs resonate with the slim oval shape of the mid-century rosewood table. While comfort is always the number one priority, a sculptural chair becomes another form of art in the room – the seductive curve of a classic Hans Wegner Wishbone chair, for example, will always work just as well in a heritage house as in a modern pied-à-terre.

Hanging a striking painting, contemporary photograph or embellished textile on the wall also helps to tell the story of who you are or where you dream to be. Even furniture elements can contribute to building a mood, like tucking a vintage bar cart from the 1950s into the corner – dressed up with all you need to whip up the perfect dirty martini – or piling up a glass-fronted armoire with bottles of the finest champagne.

Having fun with a lavish tablescape is another way to create alternative moods according to the season or occasion. I always have a few different sets of dinnerware, cutlery, candlesticks, vases, tablecloths and napkins to play around with. It is amazing the impact you can make by switching up the theme through different colours of table linen and flowers, laid out in a variety of vases and vessels or combined with a trail of fruit running along the centre of the table.

Even when a dining table isn't being used, don't leave it devoid of detail. Think about it as you would a coffee table or console, where you can play out moods inspired by other cultures and periods, lending the room a richness and depth even when empty. By creating a vignette of the things you love – stacks of books, a vase of flowers, a sculpture or hand-thrown bowl – you give the room an ongoing narrative that keeps it feeling alive, whether people are in the room or not. There should always be a sense of discovery, even if it's just a brief moment of joy when you happen to catch sight of the interior out of the corner of your eye as you walk by.

Styling a tablescape combines my love of
theatre, food and flowers. By simply mixing
and matching the different elements within
the confines of a dining table, I can tell a
never-ending series of stories according to the
celebration or season.

This page and opposite: I chose the Iksel
D-Dream wallpaper because it would wrap
a vista of stylised flora and fauna around the
dining room, reminiscent of an 18th-century
tapestry. Against this backdrop, my goal is
always to create a story on the table that fuses
flowers, foliage, fruit and vegetables, linens,
candles, vessels, glassware and cutlery in a
scene reminiscent of a Dutch still life.

This ebonised 18th-century oak armoire
boldly highlights the white vessels and
dinnerware stored inside while at the same
time creating a 'picture within a picture' effect
which speaks to the panoramic scene behind.
/
Opposite: The hues found in the wallpaper
dictated the colour palette of the brass and
tan leather bar trolley and the linen curtain in
a dusty shade of bottle green.

I love the interplay of antique and modern. In this harbourside home, I styled the owners' existing dining table by stripping it back to the raw timber and then repolishing it, teaming it with contemporary rattan and timber chairs. I accessorised with an antique Japanese urn juxtaposed with a contemporary Christophe Delcourt marble vase.

/

Opposite: The dining table can make a bold statement even when it is not set. The tall wooden candelabras and vase of towering Japanese maple foliage along with the wire chandeliers floating aloft create a breathtaking vista at any time of the day.

The sumptuous garden landscape surrounding this house dictated that we keep the internal styling very simple. A streamlined table, serpentine tubular chairs and an oversized terracotta urn filled with a glossy banana palm seamlessly complement the lush, verdant feel of the outdoors.

'Having fun with a **LAVISH TABLESCAPE** *is another way to create alternate* **MOODS** *according to the* **SEASON** *or* **OCCASION**.'

I love playing with layers to trick the eye and give a submersive feel. Here, I often bring in foliage, fruit and flowers that purposely echo the exotic mood set by the wallpaper.

/

Opposite: You can bring drama to the simplest of surfaces, especially at Christmas, my favourite time of year to style the home. A simple chrome tray table is lent some Hollywood glamour with an abundance of fragrant pine branches, ripe pears and Wedgwood crystal glasses, ready and waiting for corks to pop as guests arrive.

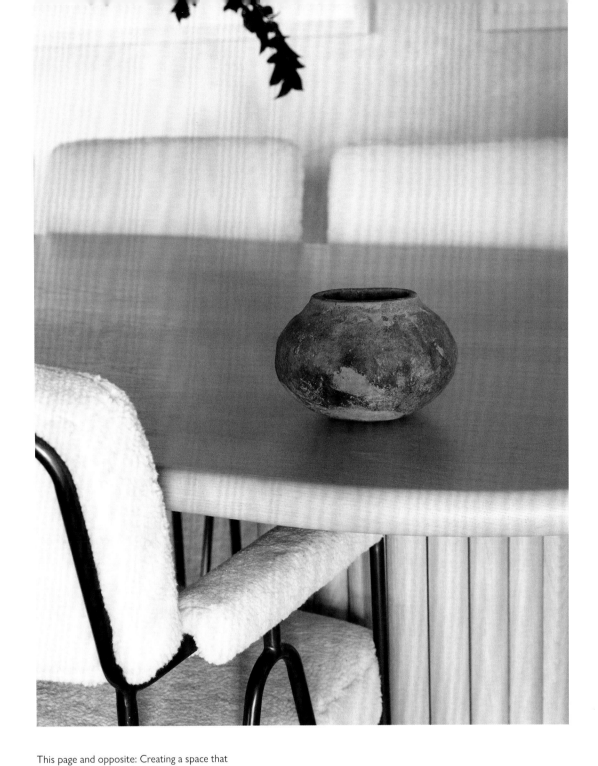

This page and opposite: Creating a space that delights the eye as a whole but comes to life in each individual detail is the success and joy of styling any room. Layering marble, bronze, wool, bouclé, glass, ceramic, terracotta and timber, playing them off each other in terms of silhouette and tone, lends the dining room of this beachside home designed by Alexander & Co. a multi-dimensional feel while maintaining a sense of relaxed composure.

In this calming space designed by Hugh-Jones Mackintosh, every element speaks to the others. From the steel-hued dining chairs to the mesmerising seascape by Chris Langlois and the ebullient ball of hydrangeas, each detail tells its own individual story while harmonising with the narrative of the room as a whole.
/
Opposite: Green marble, tan leather, cobalt linen and a graphic jungle print create a comforting morning nook just off the kitchen in this harbourside home designed by Arent&Pyke.

This Murano vase is a styling staple of mine, for its elegant structure as well as its handmade detail. It works as perfectly with flowers as with foliage, or even on its own.
/
Opposite: There is a playfulness to the layering of pieces in this dining space designed by Arent&Pyke, from the Nonggirrnga Marawili textile on the wall to the Nelson Saucer crisscross bubble pendant, which makes it feel eclectic and worldly but welcoming at the same time.

Linearity is a huge part of styling. This bar nook plays off the clean lines of the marble door frame and the rectangular brass and glass trolley, but excites the eye with its clustered arrangement of bottles, glasses and flowers.
/
Opposite: The starting point for this dining space in an inner city apartment was the brass metal pendant I found at a flea market in Paris. This chimes well with the stained timber table, vintage Thonet chairs and the spikiness of the black cockatoo's feathers in Leila Jeffreys' photograph.
/
Overleaf: This spring-themed tablescape comes to life with one of my favourite palettes of fresh white and green. Bamboo cutlery, gold-rimmed glassware, floral motif Ralph Lauren Home dinnerware and embroidered linen feel fresh alongside vases filled with scented roses and lily of the valley, bowls of lemons and ceramic candlesticks.

DURABLE DUALITY Style a space with things that can be both useful and attractive. I like the duality of accessories where something can look great by itself but can also function in practical terms as a vase, plate or serving platter. Have cleverly thought-through objects and accessories to hand, as these are great tools for styling memorable tablescapes.

A LIVED LIFE For a space to feel layered and multifaceted it needs to have a sense of history. Adding an antique Chinese or Japanese vessel, a worn timber console or chair, or an old silver tray – each full of old soul – lends another layer of texture and tone to a space, playing off its otherwise cleaner lines, as well as providing a sense of place and travel.

STYLISH ENTERTAINING 101 Even if I am having a few friends over for a casual Sunday dinner, I always have one clear concept in mind to carry through the whole event. It could be as simple as using the dish that kick-started the menu to filter through to the flowers on the table, deciding what space to host the gathering in, the music to play and even the scent to subtly burn in the background. This conceptual 'mood board' brings all the best elements of a gathering together: food, music, tablescaping, drinks and even what you will wear.

FAVOURITE TABLETOP SOURCES I pick up old and new pieces wherever I travel, but in Paris I love **Simrane** (simrane.com) for handcrafted Indian textiles, from quilts and tablecloths to cushions, and the ever-evolving lifestyle collections at **Merci Paris** (merci-merci.com). In New York, I love the quirkiness and originality of the pieces at **John Derian** in the East Village (johnderian.com), as well as the kitchen staples and homewares at **Williams Sonoma** (williams-sonoma.com) and **Crate & Barrel** (crateandbarrel.com). In the UK, I always head to the one-stop **Daylesford Farm** shop in the Cotswolds (daylesford.com) for everything chic and understated, from linen tablecloths in soft hues to wooden cooking spoons and chopping boards. In Italy, I seek out handmade ceramics by **Ceramiche Mennella**, Ischia's oldest ceramics shop (mennella.it), and **Ceramiche Nicola Fasano** in Puglia (fasanocnf.it). At home, I am always scouring **Greene & Greene** in Sydney for antique silverware (greeneandgreene.com.au) and seeking out colourtastic serving bowls and jugs at **Dinosaur Designs** (dinosaurdesigns.com.au). Online, I look for unusual finds from around the world at **Moda Operandi** (modaoperandi.com) and vintage pieces via **Etsy** (etsy.com).

DREAM DINNER PARTY Beyoncé (to delve into her incredible creative process); Maya Angelou (for her wisdom); Oprah (because, Oprah); the late Queen Elizabeth II (to ask if I can visit behind the scenes in her palaces); Elsie de Wolfe (for her brilliant decorating insights and gossip about the legendary parties she used to throw); and John Pawson (to learn more about his minimalist design ethos); and my friend Donna Hay, (to whip up my favourite chocolate fudge cake with ganache icing).

MUSIC A great playlist is essential for inspiring the right mood, whether it is humming away in the background while you are cooking up a storm in the kitchen or creating the perfect atmosphere for entertaining family and friends over a long languid lunch or a dressed-up dinner party.

Some of my favourite tunes to spin: Via Con Me – Paolo Conte; Quando, Quando, Quando – Tony Renis; Parole Parole – Mina; Volare – Domenico Modugno; Sway (Quien Sera) – Dean Martin; Buona Sera – Louis Prima; Mambo Italiano – Carla Boni; 'S Wonderful – Diana Krall; Everything Happens to Me – Samara Joy; Yes Sir, That's My Baby – Etta Jones; It Might as Well be Spring – Caity Gyorgy feat. Kyle Pogline; Stompin' at the Savoy – Teddy Wilson; All Of You – Ella Fitzgerald; It Don't Mean A Thing (If It Ain't Got That Swing) – Ernestine Anderson; It Had To Be You – Bobby Darin; Cheek to Cheek – Sammy Davis Jr. & Carmen McRae; Get Happy – Rebecca Ferguson; You Send Me – Sam Cooke … and anything from the soundtracks of Nancy Meyers' films *Something's Gotta Give* and *It's Complicated*.

WONDROUS WALLPAPERS Boyac (boyac. com.au) for a curated collection of the world's leading fabric, wallpaper and passementerie brands, including De le Cuona, Métaphores and Thibaut; **Phillip Jeffries** (phillipjeffries. com) for gloriously graphic and innovative wall coverings; Glamora (glamora.it) for lining walls with powerful contemporary motifs inspired by nature; **Calico Wallpaper** (calicowallpaper. com) for atmospheric, otherworldly wallpaper grounded in the ancient techniques of paper marbling; **De Gournay** (degournay.com) for intricate bespoke scenes, traditional and modern, informed by the hand painted and finished art of chinoiserie; **Porter's Paints** (porterspaints.com) for bold narratives and global brands such as Designers Guild, House of Hackney and Osborne & Little; **Ralph Lauren Home** (ralphlauren. com) for a preppy, sportif American vibe; **Elliott Clarke** (elliottclark.com.au) for a vibrant edit of the world's best boutique brands, including Anna Spiro, Ottoline, Fermoie and Michael S Smith Inc. **Cole & Son** (cole-and-son.com) for historical and contemporary wallpapers, including Fornasetti's iconic whimsical patterns.

A mini wildflower meadow running along the centre of the table, accompanied by piles of green pears and tranches of moss, sets the scene for this table setting featuring hand-painted glasses, silver cutlery and Dior Lily of the Valley plates decorated with a gentle *toile de jouy* motif.

V

Calm

The Bedroom

The bedroom is the soul of a home. It is the room that needs to feel particularly personal, private and protective. Calm, not cluttered, tailored yet luxurious, and with an appealing softness that comes with the gentle layering of colour, tactile materials and ambient lighting. It doesn't have to be frou-frou or flouncy; bedrooms can still be simple and clean lined, but edges and finishes shouldn't feel too hard. I like bedrooms to be well edited so there is a sense of clarity, which is not only visually pleasing, but also sets up the basic function of a bedroom – a place to rest. However, this doesn't mean a bedroom is bland. How you design and style it should reflect your truest personality.

The choice of fabric for the bedhead and the colour of the bedlinen can provide the perfect starting point for how to decorate the rest of the room. I consider navy, indigo blue and deep green to be as much neutrals as I do greys, creams and white. In a guest bedroom at Rosedale, I used an earthy hemp wallpaper in spicy ochre as the neutral, allowing the tropical feel of the floral fabric upholstering the headboard to stand out as the star of the show. In one of the guest houses, I opted for a pared-back, European farmhouse feel, where the soft drape of white bedlinen, the pale taupe of the upholstered headboard and the chalkiness of limewashed brick walls provided a soothing foil for the warmth of the herringbone-patterned terracotta tiled floor, the exposed wooden beams and rustic bedside tables.

The aim is to create the most decadent, cosseting bed possible: a headboard that is padded and softly upholstered; fresh, crisp linen; a duvet big enough to hang over the sides of the bed, but which stops just short of the floor; two or four bed pillows to add support and height; a tactile throw, blanket or quilt to layer in a contrasting texture; and as many scatter cushions as you fancy, perfect for enhancing the room's theme of colour or pattern, whether tonally or with interesting finishes like fringed edges or embroidery. If possible, line walls with a grasscloth or paper-backed linen to soften the room's acoustics, and install low-level lighting via table and floor lamps rather than overhead spotlights, because this will instantly create an encompassing mood.

Rugs should also feel generous; they don't need to simply mirror the footprint of the bed, and even if you have carpet, layer another rug over the top to mark out different zones in the room. Layering in all those material moments – a wool or shaggy silk rug over a sisal carpet, for example – makes a bedroom feel just that bit warmer.

Where there is space, I love to transform a corner of a bedroom into an intimate breakout area, bringing in a comfy lounge chair, ottoman and small table; perfect for cosying up with a mug of coffee and the weekend papers, or a glass of wine and a good book, or simply as a chill-out zone where you can watch the day go by outside. The top of a chest of drawers offers an ideal styling moment that can also be practical: an antique vanity mirror, a piece of artwork resting against the wall, a cool retro record player or vintage-style Roberts radio, an exquisite marquetry box holding jewellery, makeup or watches – it all adds to the pampering mood.

I also like to thread the idea of ritual through the design and feel of a bedroom. On my bedside table is an oil burner, a water carafe and glass, and a stick of sage which I burn to cleanse the energy in the air as part of my daily routine. You might include a chair onto which you can sling your clothes at the end of a long day; a bedside cabinet drawer where you keep not just lotions and potions but cables for charging your phone overnight; a clock, water glass and notebook that sit on the bedside table. Having personal mementos – a framed photograph, a pile of pebbles picked up on a beach while on holiday, a vintage dish found at a flea market for keeping your reading glasses safe – are often things people don't consider having on display by the bed.

I think there should always be a posy of flowers or leaves picked straight from the garden to add freshness and life, and a table lamp with a sculptural feel to provide further visual interest, as well as light. It is important to be surrounded by the things you genuinely love, especially as they are the first thing you will see in the morning and the last thing you will see at night.

This page and opposite: A bedroom should always feel personal and inviting, using bedlinen, lamps, mirrors, rugs, artwork and sentimental objects to create a peaceful mood. For me, a bedroom should evoke a spirit of calm, so I always opt for a neutral scheme layered with subtle textures and geometrics, which still intrigues the eye while remaining restful.

This page and opposite: In one of the guest cottages at Rosedale, there is depth in the layers of tactile materials, from slubby linen upholstering the enclosing bedhead and crisp monogrammed cotton pillowcases to the studded leather armchair, worn wooden bench and woven area rug overlaying the herringbone tiled floor.

In this bedroom designed by Arent&Pyke, the amber orchids speak to the ochre trim of the curtains, bringing interest into an otherwise neutrally hued space.

/

Opposite: Depending on space, a simple seating vignette lends a 'room-within-room' feel to a bedroom, providing somewhere to unwind, meditate or simply decompress after a busy day.

'The aim is to create
the most DECADENT,
COSSETING BED *possible* …
*it all adds to the pampering
mood of the room.*'

Monogrammed detailing on towels, pillowcases and even slippers lends everyday accessories an elegant five-star hotel feel.
/
Opposite: Much like a powder room, a guest bedroom can be somewhere to play more directionally with style. I wanted to instil a hint of the tropics into this guest room, teaming a paper-backed flax linen wallpaper, antique English oak commode and a curvaceous bedside lamp with a bedhead upholstered in Lisa Fine Textiles' refined Pasha palm print.

An intricately quilted bedspread in pure white
is the easiest way to style a bed so it looks crisp
and tailored. It is also my go-to 'bedroom-ready'
trick, easily layered with scatter cushions and
throws in accent colours and motifs depending
on the season.
/
Opposite: This fabric-panelled bedhead designed
by Morgan Ferry is not only comforting and
cocooning but also clever, its slim ledge doubling
as a gallery for displaying art and objects.

This page and opposite: Another guest room at Rosedale was designed for when nieces and nephews come to stay. I drew inspiration from Ralph Lauren's smart and chic preppy style – a constant reference point for me – as I wanted it to feel playful and bold, but cosy as well. I started with a navy grasscloth wallpaper by Porter's Paints as the first layer, before bringing in pieces like the striped twin bedheads and cushions, antique rug and Georgian campaign chest. I added a contemporary photograph of an Eastern grass owl by Leila Jeffreys, brass bedside lights and fun objects such as a vintage cricket bat.

With magnificent ocean views dominating this principal bedroom by Mim Design, it seemed best to opt for tonal and textural material choices that didn't compete, but blended with the surrounding landscape.

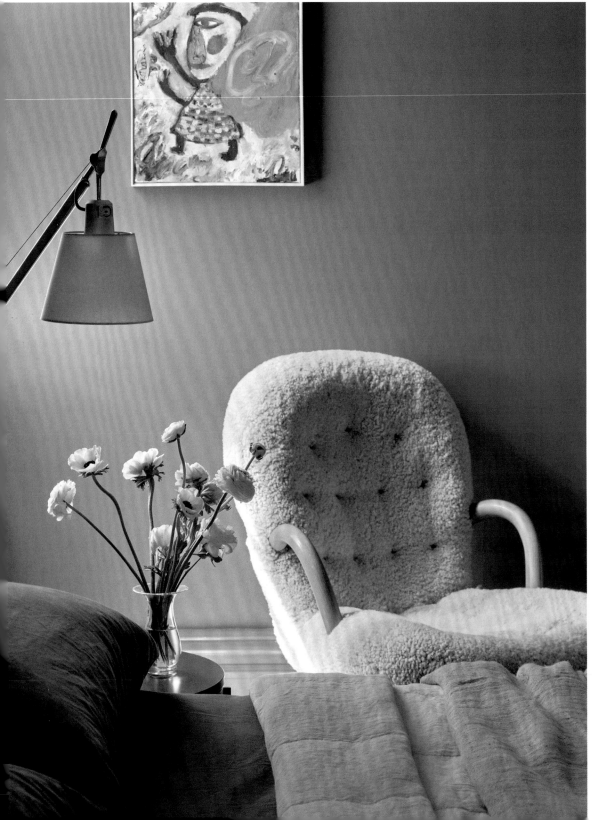

Rich, bold but feel-good materials stand out here. A bouclé-covered Philip Arctander Clam chair, contemporary artwork by John Edwards, and ochre-hued linen sheets work empathetically in this bedroom nook styled for Arent&Pyke.
/
Opposite: The frenetic frequency of the geometric fabric upholstering the bedhead works as a vibrant artwork of sorts, but feels calmed by the antique rug and the ochre Society Limonta linen.

The smallest of details – a golden glazed
ceramic Aerin vase filled with scented
roses and a shagreen clock – can create a
special moment in any bedroom nook.
/
Opposite: The design for my favourite
bedroom at home was inspired by one in
acclaimed designer Rose Uniacke's London
townhouse, where multiple shades of white
jostle to create a feeling of serene sanctuary.

The grandeur of this bedroom is enhanced by the floor-to-ceiling antique bronze silk curtains, the muted tonal rug and textural abstract painting, while the boldness of the black and white linen, bedside tables and high-gloss lamps add a contemporary touch. Styled for Morgan Ferry Design.

Positioning a graphic black and white photograph by Joshua Yeldham within the wall panelling above the bedhead plays with proportion to create a dramatic focal point for the space. The monochromatic palette segues from the bedding to the bedside table and lamp.

/

Opposite: This is one of my all-time favourite styling moments, where a simple white bedcover, contemporary Tizio lamps designed by Richard Sapper for Artemide and sleekly minimal bedside tables contrast with the antique tapestry hanging above the bed, reminiscent of the stylistic scenes in the film *Call Me by Your Name*. Styled for Arent&Pyke.

LUXURIOUS LINENS Julia B. Casa, Florence (juliab.com) is possibly my favourite store in the world, purveyor of the most intricately embroidered, appliquéd and trimmed bed, bath and table linens, as well as hand-painted tableware, hand-wrought silverware, hand-crocheted lampshades, retro outdoor furniture and vintage glass, with a very special monogramming service. I also love **Society Limonta** (societylimonta.com) for the finest quality household linens in natural neutrals.

BEST WEEKEND RITUAL My favourite weekends in Sydney start with a green smoothie, then walking the dogs around the harbour, a beach swim, afternoon movie then dinner at favourite spots in Potts Point, like Cho Cho San for Japanese (chochosan.com.au) or Fratelli Paradiso for Italian (fratelliparadiso.com). At the farm, I am up early tending to the animals, opening the poultry house and watering the garden beds on rotation for that day, before heading to town to shop at my favourite organic grocer or the Saturday farmer's market. If there is a rare afternoon off, I love to head to Fourth Crossing waterfalls in the Mullion Range State Conservation Area, followed by a meal in the outdoor kitchen at home or at Hey Rosey (heyrosey.com.au), The Union Bank (theunionbank.com.au) or Printhie Wines (printhiewines.com.au) in the nearby town of Orange.

GUILTY PLEASURES Pasta and gelato; investing in luggage (overnight bags, totes, suitcases, keepalls and duffels); and collecting scented candles everywhere I travel: Trudon, Jo Malone London, Santa Maria Novella, Diptyque, St. Rose, Le Labo, Aerin, Byredo, Maison Margiela, Nette, Tom Ford, Maison Louis Marie, Loewe, Dior, Lola James Harper, Paul Smith, Acqua Di Parma. The list goes on … and on … and on.

MORE IS MORE If you have a complete obsession with throw cushions, as I do, the rule is the more the merrier. Scatter cushions are a great way to layer interesting graphics and motifs into any bedroom scheme.

BEDROOM RITUALS By my bed, I always have a table lamp, a vase of flowers or greenery, a water carafe and drinking glass, scenting elements (a bowl of Palo Santo wood sticks or a bundle of sage to burn), a trinket box and a crystal (I use white quartz to help hold and amplify intention while diffusing an aura of tranquillity and peace).

SOOTHING TEXTURES I enjoy dressing the bed in crisp, white Italian linen, which can then easily be transformed from season to season with a different duvet or set of cushions. I also love using velvet for upholstering a bedhead, to use as a trim for cushions, or as generous floor-length drapes – it instantly envelops the room in a luxurious richness.

THINGS I CAN'T LIVE WITHOUT There are the obvious things: my dogs and family of course. But day to day, I couldn't live without meditation, music and the ability to create – even if that means simply putting fresh flowers in a vase, moving a bowl from the left side of the coffee table to the right, or fluffing the cushions a different way while making the bed. I need to be creative in some small way every single day. Like oxygen, it sustains me.

IF I WERE A COLOUR OR A PIECE OF ART I would be either a crisp white or soft cool-toned flax, or an antique Italian bust.

FAVOURITE PAINTS
Porter's Paints (porterspaints.com): Popcorn (a crisp white that provides the perfect canvas); Aniseed (my all-time favourite black); Black Cockatoo (a dark charcoal with an olive undertone used for Rosedale's kitchen joinery).
Dulux (dulux.com): Lexicon Quarter (a cool fresh white); Tranquil Retreat (a soft romantic grey); Juvenile (a deep, sexy grey).
Bauwerk Colour (bauwerkcolour.com): Chickpea (a beautiful limewash finish in a mid-tone neutral).
Farrow & Ball (farrow-ball.com): Off-Black (a deep soft black); Wevet (a delicate mid-tone white that doesn't throw any yellow); Bamboozle (a fiery flame red).
Benjamin Moore (benjaminmoore.com): Alabaster (a fresh, crisp white with a tiny touch of pink); Smokey Taupe (a warmish mid-grey).
Portola (portolapaints.com): Lisbon (a muted seafoam grey).
Clare (clare.com): Daily Greens (a mossy olive green).
Rose Uniacke (roseuniacke.com): Toffee (a rich oxide red); Dune (an earthy caramel); Cotton (a calming faint grey).

In this white and blue tailored bedroom, well-worn pieces such as a Chinese elmwood bench at the end of the bed, a Turkish urn sitting between the windows and a Persian Aleph flatweave rug add a well-lived, well-travelled resonance to the room.

VI

Unwind

My one rule when designing a bathroom is to make it feel like a space you want to relax in. I draw on ideas from hotels and luxurious bedrooms for elements to add that will make a bathing space feel more like a living space. This includes rugs, lighting, curtains, art, mirrors and even upholstered furniture, like a charming antique buttoned 'nursing' chair to sit on while you towel down or moisturise after a shower or bath. These are the little details that make a bathroom feel truly special.

At Rosedale, I wanted to make the main bathroom feel grand and glamorous while harmonising with the overall colour palette of the house. One of the starting points was a beautiful 18th-century French-style gilded and ebonised cabinet I came across at an antique store. I had thought I would have this retro-fitted with a couple of basins, but in the end it was just too costly, so I found a great company who makes something similar at a much better price. I then teamed this with a classic Carrara marble top, brass taps and handles, complemented by a pair of large ornate gilded mirrors.

For me, the best way to inject personality into a bathroom space is to play with the accessories, especially from season to season. I love to switch out the towels, and experiment with scents – whether it is an enticingly perfumed candle or diffuser, or even just a heavenly fragranced soap in a dish. This adds another layer of sensuality to the bathroom space that can work both to calm the nerves in the evening and lift the spirits in the morning.

In one recent bathroom I styled, the floor was laid with an octagonal mosaic tile pattern I designed as part of my Labyrinth collection for Di Lorenzo Tiles. The pattern was inspired by the myriad decorative iron grates covering windows and doors that I spotted while on a trip around Italy. I wanted to create a geometric pattern that would bring a sense of movement to a space while at the same time feel grounding. I think of tiling on the floor as being almost like a rug – it can be a great way to introduce graphic repetition into a room while keeping walls, ceiling and woodwork plain and the hardware clean-lined and classic, usually in unlacquered brass, which pleasingly ages and changes with use.

In bathrooms I even like to play with generous swathes of curtain. For example, a waterproof linen draped from ceiling to floor either side of a window, or pulled across a nice rod as a shower screen, lends finesse to a bathroom's proportions. On shelves or vanity counters I always arrange curvaceous vases filled with an abundance of flowers or glossy green leaves from the garden or local florist, often teamed with other quirky vessels found on my travels. I hang art in bathrooms too – being mindful that the room has adequate ventilation and protecting the paintings or prints from humidity by applying a layer of acrylic glass over the regular glass and choosing metal or acrylic frames, which are more resilient to moisture than wood.

Similar to how we think about cushions and throws in a bedroom or on a sofa, think of towels and mats as those interchangeable elements that can make a bathroom tell different stories through the year. You might choose something vivid with a zigzag Missoni print, maybe an elegantly monogrammed design, or perhaps a soft, handwoven Turkish cotton with a textural, raw edge in earthy tones that brings out the pigment in a handmade wall tile. And don't forget about all those practical elements – soap, shampoo, hand wash, cotton wool balls – which can be stored in beautiful glass bottles or ceramic jars to add further interest to the bathroom's narrative.

These are the details that soften a bathroom and make it feel more personal. It makes you want to spend time there, whether taking a long bath, doing your makeup, or giving yourself a pampering facial – it encourages you to slow down and be kind to yourself.

This page and opposite: The most indulgent material for any bathroom is natural marble or stone. Carrara marble in this beachside home is softened with textures including a Chinese elm stool and matte ceramic vase, with an accent of sage green bath products. To evoke a luxurious European hotel feel, a stack of fluffy white towels, artisan bath products, fresh flowers and a focus on lighting create a relaxed, indulgent mood.
/
Overleaf: In a contemporary inner-city bathroom designed by Hugh-Jones Mackintosh, the styling elements – including soft linen towels and bottles of favourite beauty lotions – echo the clean lines and graphic shapes of the rectangular mirrors, simple towel rail and bell-shaped wall lights.

Statement vintage lighting adds interesting form and texture as well as a sense of heritage to any space, especially a bathroom. Keeping things ordered – grouping everyday skincare, fragrances and soaps on a tray, complemented with a vase of flowers or foliage – ensures essentials will always be directly at hand. Styled for Hugh-Jones Macintosh.
/
Opposite: A bathroom styled for Morgan Ferry Design provides the perfect escape for unwinding after a busy day. It is easy to create little moments of sanctuary: a bowl filled with therapeutic bath essences on top of a stool set within easy reach of the bathtub, or a small bench on which to rest each foot as you dry off, are guaranteed to bring ease and pleasure to your bathtime routine.

Bath towels in contrasting shades to the tiles and floor can add a frisson of drama to any bathroom. Styled for Hugh-Jones Mackintosh.
/
Opposite: Just as you would accessorise a living room or bedroom, introducing interesting pieces such as a vintage Italian vase, beautiful bath products by Florentine brand Santa Maria Novella and a classic vintage shave set into a smart modern bathroom lends a softening sense of European elegance to the space. Styled for Arent&Pyke.

Symmetry brings serenity to the main bathroom at Rosedale, where an ebonised vanity cabinet with double sinks is paired with matching gilded mirrors and light sconces.
/
Opposite: When I created the campaign for my Labyrinth collection of bespoke marble mosaic tiles for Di Lorenzo Tiles, I used the Transition pattern to create a bold bathroom that felt more like a dressing room.

This page and opposite: A bathroom can be as glamorous as any other room in the home. From the very outset when designing this bathroom, I was determined to have dramatic curtains, so my friend Morgan from Simple Studio chose this electrum gold waxed cotton, and even now they are still my favourite curtains in the house. An antique chair provides somewhere to put extra towels or to hang a bathrobe and pyjamas; the rug makes padding from the shower to the vanity unit a comforting experience.

'The best way to INJECT
PERSONALITY *into a bathroom*
space is to PLAY *with the*
ACCESSORIES.'

This page and opposite: Gilded detailing lends a bathroom an unexpected touch of sophistication. Ornately framed mirrors talk to the natural brass of the taps, which in turn speak to the metallic detailing of bathroom shelves, antique towel rails and accessories on the vanity. A vintage leather trunk, this one by Goyard, also provides another decorative layer as well as stylish storage.

Harmonious styling, with dark grey towels and white ceramic accessories complementing the mottled pattern of the marble used for the walls and vanity unit, brings a sense of balance and grace to this bathroom. Styled for Stafford Architecture.

This page and opposite: The bold veining of the Arabescato Vagli marble used in this harbourside home introduces movement to the slimline space without overwhelming it. A small side table by the bathtub is perfect for resting a book, candle or glass of wine; while the ceramic vessels, lining the windowsill, infuse a sense of softening charm.

This page and opposite: Natural brass is one of my favourite metallic accents because it ages beautifully over time. In one of the guest house bathrooms at the farm, I custom- designed the vanities with curved ribbed detailing, topped with marble, because I loved the softness of their shape contrasted with the strength of the brass-panelled shower screen.

This page and opposite: Powder rooms present an opportunity to be whimsical and playful. I used Iksel's Kubilai's Tent wallpaper with a custom-made ceiling panel at Rosedale to make people feel like they've just walked into a marquee in Rajasthan. Rather than using typical bathroom storage, I prefer antique pieces that work practically but also add personality and a hint of the unexpected.

SWEET SCENT-SATIONS I love a scented floral moment in the bathroom – my go-to is a little vase filled with gardenias, David Austin tea roses, lilac, hyacinths and sweet *Daphne*. Otherwise, soft greenery from the garden or local market lasts longer and also feels fresh and clean in a bathroom.

POWERFUL POWDER ROOMS Powder rooms are the perfect spots to be bold and theatrical because they're usually small compact spaces, like the area under a staircase. I wanted the powder room at Rosedale to be unexpected and playful. The walls are lined with a paper from Iksel which I fell in love with as I walked past their outpost in Paris. As with the dining room mural, I wanted this to be something of a conversation piece. I've long been obsessed with the enclosing intimacy that a tent-style space creates. The ceiling was custom built and I added the tasselled bunting trims and brassy tulip wall sconces to marry with the mirror and give a carnival pavilion feel. I love that you walk in and feel as though you've stepped into a different place and time.

TERRIFIC TRANSFORMATIONS I like looking at how pieces of furniture can be used for a different use than their original intended purpose. An English oak commode can be transformed into a powder room vanity, or an antique French balustrade can be adapted as a base for a console with the addition of a custom-made marble top.

ELEVATED ELEMENTS There are only a few surfaces you can play with in a bathroom – the floor, the walls and the vanity unit – so I always consider how I can make them feel different yet in conversation with one another. I play with the architectural details: applying beaded panelling to a bathroom's walls where I might ordinarily have used tiles; introducing elements like a patterned screen (perhaps lined with a Fornasetti wallpaper or padded with a vibrant fabric) that you would otherwise find in a bedroom or study; and using industrial-style Crittall steel doors to divide a walk-in shower from the rest of the space while maintaining a sense of transparency so that light can happily flow through.

SWITCH IT UP Textiles – like towels, bathmats and wash cloths – can be a way of bringing texture and contrast into a bathroom, adding a bold splash of colour or enhancing the shimmer of a hand-glazed Zellige tile. My favourite sources for bathroom linens include **Frette** (frette.com), **Bemboka** (bemboka.com), **Cultiver** (cultiver.com.au), **C&C Milano** (cec-milano.com) and **Hale Mercantile Co**. (halemercantileco.com).

BATHROOM RITUALS I love to make the bathroom feel like I'm staying in a hotel: fluffy white towels, artisan soaps, a scented candle, magnesium salt flakes decanted into a beautiful glass jar or ceramic pot, a room spray and music softly filtering through with a gentle jazz or R&B vibe.

NATURAL PATINA Homes should always be alive, not just in terms of people but also materials, so I never really use anything that isn't natural. A terracotta urn, a marble-topped table, a glazed linen and a silky wool rug are items that not only feel grounding in a room, but they also resonate with the many hands that have helped to make them. Even though my spaces are highly curated, they never feel precious because there is always a sense of comfort threaded through that makes you feel welcome.

DECORATING LESSONS LEARNED Never to blindly follow trends or copy a look that someone else has, which may not work in your home. Our homes are the most intimate and personal representation of who we are, and everything you touch should be a moment to showcase this.

The feel for the main bathroom at Rosedale
was 'grand European hotel'. The hero was
the marble bathtub from Apaiser, while the
panelling behind echoes the wall detailing used
throughout the house. I love how the handsome
black steel frames contrast with the crisp white
walls and gold accents.

VII

Conquer

The way we use the office at home has changed enormously in the last few years. Our spaces have become multifunctional, to suit everything from hybrid remote working to home schooling and social interactions via Zoom. Whether you have a fully designated room, a desk against a wall in the nook of a living room, or dining table that can be converted into a makeshift working space where you can put your laptop down while you have a coffee, the aim for an office is to create somewhere that brings together all those practical things you need to get work done, but in an effortless and stylish way.

Naturally, an office needs to feel ordered and calm, but it doesn't have to be characterless or dull. At Rosedale, my office feels very personal, and I'm surrounded by the things I love in a comfortable environment that has been enhanced by textured grasscloth on the walls and features a big, strong, sexy desk. I'm also lucky to have a breakout space with two armchairs for sitting and reading; it has become almost like a meditation space, helping provide respite from the stresses of work.

An office can often be a hybrid space. This might be as simple as having an elegantly leather-lined tray where you can store all the bits you need and then move it around the various rooms where you sit and work at home. Or, if you have a large, generous space, think about all the elements that speak not only to you and your personality, but also to your career and professional persona. The mood you create in a working space should set you up for success: inspiring and energising, helping you to feel confident and productive.

Here you can also dare to be bold in design terms. I'm thinking of the *Mad Men* vibe, where you instinctively think, yep there's stuff getting done in there! It is the absolute opposite of the current trend for hot desking, where offices have become horribly bland, ergonomically ugly and deeply uninspiring spaces. Your desk does not have to come from an office equipment supplier. While proper chair support and desk height is essential to your physical and mental wellbeing, you can still strike a balance between a stylish aesthetic and comfort.

While desk and chair create the focal point of your designated working space, it is all the other details you bring into this space that should remind you of the things you care about, and the things you aspire to achieve. A big stack of books about Hollywood directors if you're working in film, or a vintage wooden abacus if you're an accountant sets an immediate tone. A great light should not only look good but properly illuminate your desk when you're working or reading at night; a wall dressed with a dynamic piece of art, a series of intriguing plates or a mid-century wall clock will give you something joyful to look up at in between firing off emails; a tray with glasses and a carafe for water (or whiskey) or a teapot and cups lends a pleasing finishing touch, as does a tactile vessel for flowers or an evergreen plant alongside framed photos of loved ones or favourite holiday snaps.

Ideally an office needs to feel slightly more organised than other spaces – you know what they say, 'a tidy desk, a tidy mind' – so storage is also key. This might be a series of floating shelves where you can keep books, knick-knacks and smartly covered box files for paperwork; or an armoire where you can hide everything away. You can also store work detritus in chic stackable lacquered boxes or vintage Louis Vuitton trunks or you can source a desk with extra-deep drawers. Whatever you choose, one of my general rules is that your functional everyday office requirements should also work with the theme and style of your home. Everything should be interesting – a pen pot could be a beautifully hand-thrown mug, or a little Murano dish can hold paper clips and spare coins – and should tell the story of you, both your style and what you do professionally. These are the things that help kick you back into action should inspiration or confidence momentarily wane, and remind you of who you want to be and where you want to go next.

Creating small moments that remind me of my journey and capture a snapshot of my life play a key role in how I style a room at home. Here, a simple tray laden with a Trudon Reggio candle, perfume, garden roses in a crystal vase, long matches held in an Indian lassi cup and a glass-blown paperweight made by hand in the Maldives sits next to a Ralph Lauren Home frame displaying a snapshot from a trip to Paris many years ago.

/

Opposite: The office was the first room I renovated at the farm. I had such a clear vision of using Phillip Jeffries' Chevron Chic grasscloth across the walls and hanging a Ralph Lauren navy leather pendant light, teamed with an antique Chinese Peking rug from Cadrys 1952 and accents of brass and ebonised furniture to create a masculine space that felt both pleasing and powerful at the same time.

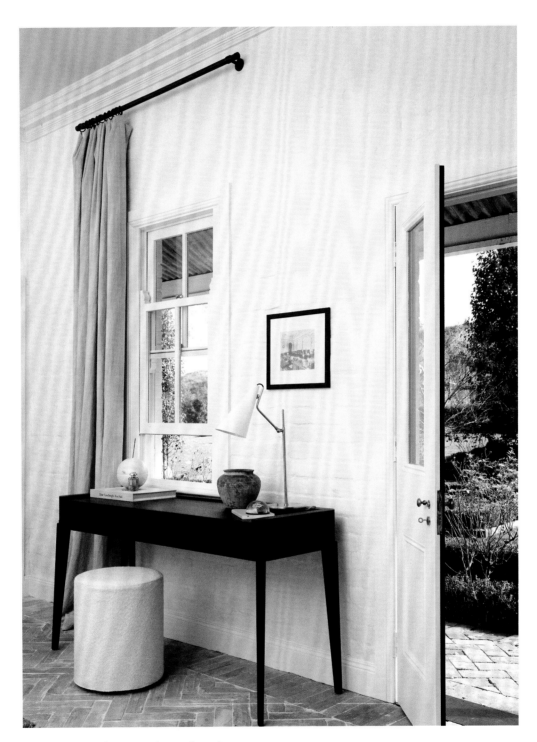

Even the smallest of spaces can be transformed
into a multi-tasking area. Here, in one of the
guest rooms at Rosedale, a streamlined table
is teamed with a lamp and stool to create the
perfect spot for sitting and catching up on
emails while enjoying the idyllic garden views
outside the window.
/
Opposite: This Melbourne office designed by
Morgan Ferry had rich textures of grasscloth,
velvet curtains and attention-grabbing artwork
by Cressida Beale, so I added in sculptural
objects, both vintage and contemporary, to the
mantel and desk to make the space feel warm
yet dynamic.

Even if you don't have enough space for a stand-alone office, a built-in or console-style desk can work under a window when styled to suit the broader elements of the room around it.
/
Opposite: Colour is the common thread that ties the different elements together in this room – from the simple vase of blue hydrangeas and the shade of duck egg blue on the walls to the cobalt tones in the artwork – and also complements the cool silver tone of the lamp and desk chair. Getting the tones right within a space is a simple way of creating harmony and connection.
/
Overleaf: One of my favourite 'non-office' office spaces is in this beachside home designed by Mim Design. A pale marble floating bench provided the perfect area to create an intermittent desk space, demarcated from the rest of the living room by an area rug and ottoman, while the contemporary objects, lamps and artwork stylistically connect the two spaces together.

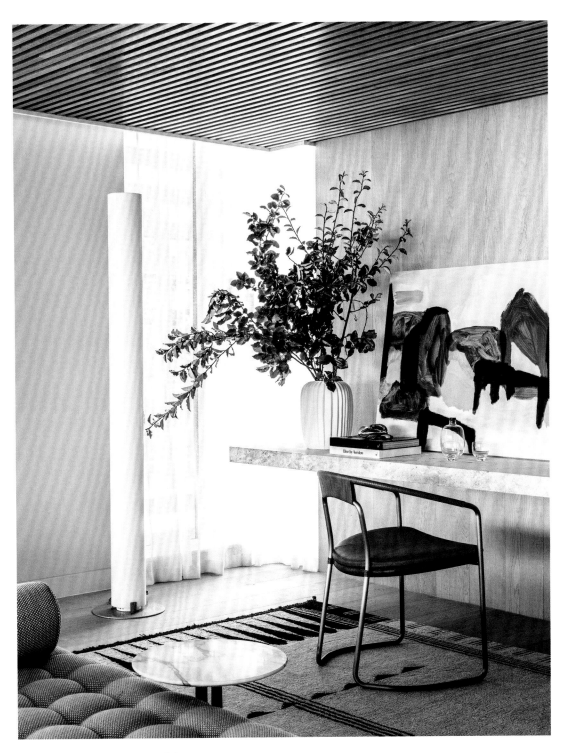

This page and opposite: The mix of elements such as a Moroccan rug, leather chair, opaque Flos 'Stylos' glass floor lamp, Guaxs vase, timber-panelled ceiling and marble benches creates a balanced alchemy of texture and form.

The direction of natural light should dictate the positioning of furniture within any space. You never want to block the source of light or add in solid elements that will dull the room's brightness.

/

Opposite and overleaf: In the first home office I designed, my starting point was the Martinique wallpaper made famous by The Beverly Hills Hotel in Los Angeles. It still feels timeless today, especially when teamed with the various vintage elements seen here, including the 1970s brass lamp and the McGuire Butterfly rattan chair by Edward Tuttle, the leather and bronze tray, and limed heavy-grained contemporary desk by James Salmond Furniture.

The charcoal grasscloth wallpaper in Morgan Ferry's country home office makes a bold backdrop for the lighter accents of the white mantelpiece, pale wood woven armchairs, black and white ceramics, and paintings by Alan Jones (centre) and Alexandra Brownlow (right).

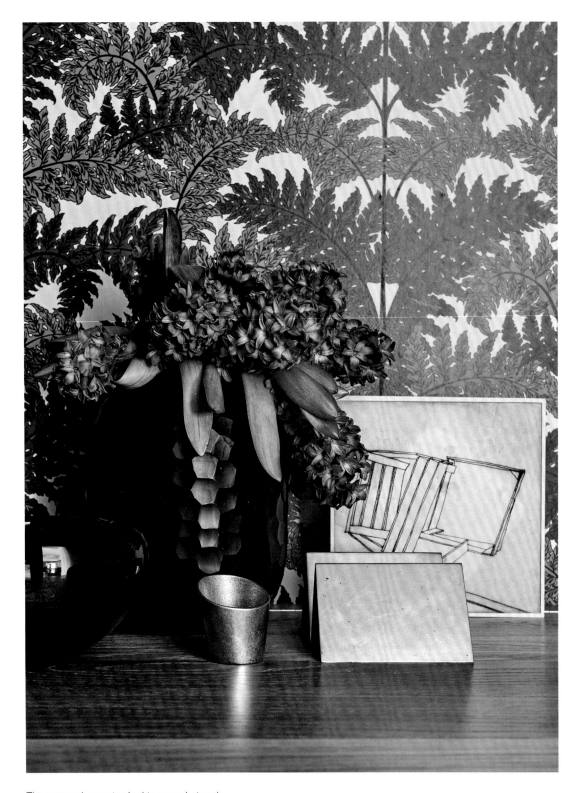

This page and opposite: In this space designed
by Arent&Pyke, a simple cluster of objects
imbued with intriguing sharp lines, including
a Guaxs vase, framed ceramic artwork and
industrial brass pieces by Henry Wilson,
creates an interesting contrast next to the
romantic fern motif of the wallpaper.

'THE MOOD *you create in a* WORKING SPACE *should set you up for success:* INSPIRING *and* ENERGISING.'

I love the simplicity of combining a few elements where each one is a statement in its own right but when grouped together they create an even more magical moment.
/
Opposite: When space allows, a statement occasional chair like this Hans J. Wegner Flag Halyard chair can feel luxurious and bold in an office space, especially when teamed with pieces like Piero Lissoni's occasional table for Cassina, embedded with a streamlined task light, and a textural rug styled with a monochromatic palette.

Never underestimate the power of a statement rug in transforming a room. An Armadillo Eden rug in citrine feels like a golden platform on which I've showcased bold-toned furniture with strong silhouettes in this office by Morgan Ferry Design.
/
Opposite: Bookshelves aren't just for books. They can be vibrant, exciting places for bringing together collected objects, sculptural forms and mementos. Here I took my cue from the tones in the Serge Mouille three-headed floor lamp and George Nelson Sunflower wall clock to inspire the colour palette of sepia, off-white and warm grey objects added to the shelves; both vintage and modern, objects are accented with gold or highlighted in crisp white.

READING MATTERS I love to reference design books for room layout and styling ideas. For inspiration for the office space at Rosedale, I turned to *Joseph Dirand: Interior,* by Jospeh Dirand and *Rose Uniacke at Work* (all Rizzoli).

OTHER FAVOURITE REFERENCES INCLUDE:
Axel Vervoordt: Portraits of Interiors (Flammarion); Ralph Lauren's *A Way of Living: Home, Design, Inspiration* (Rizzoli); *Gio Ponti* by Graziella Roccella (Taschen); Paul Bertolli's *Cooking by Hand* (Random House); Bunny Williams' *Life in the Garden* (Rizzoli); *Flower Addict* by Grandiflora's Saskia Havekes (Lantern); *The Things That Matter* by Nate Berkus (Spiegel & Grau).

STORAGE TIPS Vintage trinket boxes, lacquered or leather trays, and stacked Indian chapati boxes are great for storing and displaying office items and also suit the style aesthetic of an office space.

GO GREEN I always have a tall Kentia palm in a wicker basket or ceramic pot in the corner of the room, and a small floral moment on the desk.

BRING IN PATTERN A patterned grasscloth or geometric wallpaper works well in an office space, enabling you to be bolder with layering in a colour or pattern palette through scatter cushions, window treatments (such as blinds, shutters or curtains) or rugs.

MOST PRIZED POSSESSION The vintage Louis Vuitton trunk given to me on my thirtieth birthday.

BEST GIFT My all-time favourite gift to give is a bunch of fragrant fresh flowers accompanied by a handwritten note on personalised embossed stationery I pick up at the Milanese outpost for Florentine stationers Pineider (pineider.com).

PATIENCE IS A VIRTURE Waiting to find the perfect piece is not only a virtue, but is also crucial to making your home feel well edited, curated and layered. A home shouldn't feel like a showroom, with items chosen straight off the shop floor. It should tell a story of moments dotted throughout that start conversations or spark memories. The time it takes to find the perfect chandelier, cocktail table or bedhead isn't wasted because it takes you on a journey that allows you to explore and grow with your space rather than just making do.

MUSEUMS & GALLERIES Wherever I travel, one of my first stops is an exhibition at one of my favourite museums or galleries. In Paris, I head for the **Musée de l'Orangerie** (musee-orangerie. fr) in the Tuileries Garden to see Monet's *Water Lilies.* That space and the artwork calms me and transports me to another world that is pure magic. In New York, **MoMA** (moma.org) is always top of my list, followed by **The Metropolitan Museum of Art** (metmuseum.org) for the unforgettable fashion exhibits, often curated with a strong and, sometimes, controversial point of view. I am constantly drawn to the work of artists such as Salvador Dalí, Mark Rothko, Yayoi Kusama and Matt Bromhead.

Other must-visits include: The Uffizi, Florence (uffizi.it); Musée d'Orsay, Paris (musee-orsay.fr); Getty Museum, Los Angeles (getty.org); Mona (Museum of Old and New Art), Hobart (mona. net.au); National Gallery of Victoria, Melbourne (ngv.vic.gov.au); Museum of Contemporary Art, Sydney (mcm.com.au); Michael Reid Galleries, Sydney and Berlin (michaelreid.com.au); Olsen Gallery, Sydney (olsengallery.com); National Art School Gallery, Sydney (nas.edu.au); and the Victoria & Albert Museum, London (vam.ac.uk).

I love styling this antique English mahogany secretaire as another 'literary' space, dressed with scented candles, books and a vase of flowers. The look and feel of it transports me to a bygone era when we had the time for writing letters by hand and reading the newspaper every day.

VIII

Connect

Hallways are no longer merely lengthy passages between rooms: they should naturally join the dots from one space to the next, but also feel like enticing, enthralling spaces in their own right. I find that hallways – and also landings, stairwells, and anywhere that guides you through a house – are almost like light tunnels. People usually want to simply rush past or through them, so creating moments that invite people to pause in these areas and take an interest in what's around them feels especially rewarding.

No matter how compact these spots might be, you can easily create drama within them. For example, the area around a window can easily be forgotten, or frankly be very boring. On the first floor at Rosedale, I've turned an otherwise nothing space into a window seat, boxed out into a little banquette, which I've covered with lots of comfy cushions and accessorised with an antique bust, Persian rug and stack of books. It instantly invites you to stop and read a book as the afternoon sun streams in. In essence, I have created another living space, but one that takes in the view and has a bit of personality and a sense of place within the overall scheme of the bedrooms leading off the hall.

You can create magic in the smallest of spaces, sometimes making them even more special to discover than the grand hero moments you find in a living or dining room. You might need to think about them more, because you're playing with tighter proportions, but even the space between two doorways can be transformed. In a corner no more than a metre wide, set between a wall and doorway in the upstairs hallway at Rosedale, I placed a brushed brass lamp on top of a small console table, its round mushroom head feeling a little oversized for the width of the table, but it was balanced out with the rest of the accessories I teamed it with, including a small stack of books, a lovely bowl, a Perspex vase of flowers, an obelisk sculpture and a mini bust. It never ceases to catch my eye every time I walk by.

Transitional spaces also allow me to play around vertically: whether it is a thin corridor, a compressed corner, or an alcove underneath a staircase, I am always thinking of clever ways to draw the eye upwards. This might include sourcing a dazzling pendant light for a small hallway that makes you instantly look up and see the intricate decorative cornicing, or hanging a series of mirrors to maximise the amount of light bouncing around the space. Equally, creating a gallery-style moment along a wall with a series of framed paintings or prints, or laying a long, vibrant runner along a corridor floor also helps to transport people through a space.

For one slim hallway, leading from a front door to an open-plan living space at the back of the house, I found a vintage Italian console from the 1960s that was very skinny but also sculptural. It has just enough space to accommodate a voluptuous vase, a couple of objects and a keepsake box, and is complemented with a simple circular mirror above and dramatic wall lights by Apparatus hung either side (which speak to the larger version hanging as a pendant in the entrance). Here, playing with sculpture, form and proportions fires the imagination in a way that leaving a corridor white and empty never could.

Given that you might walk down a hallway many times a day, why shouldn't it be interesting? For me, this is part of the joy of what I do, finding ways to reverse the thinking about purely transitional spaces – they can be styled to exude their own narrative, making you want to stop, linger and dream.

Fragrance in a hallway helps to create an alluring but intangible sensory moment that often stops you in your tracks and makes you appreciate the space you are walking through.
/
Opposite: My love for bold statement greenery works perfectly in a hallway because it is usually a tall, narrow space and can take the height of the arrangement. Here, elongated branches of foliage such as English elm, oak and smoke bush help draw the eye upwards, encouraging you to notice the detailing of the top of the elaborately carved antique mirror and the historic cornicing of the late 19th-century house.

My favourite spot for seeking out a quiet moment
of respite at home is the banquette at the end of
the upstairs hallway. The arrangement of cushions
from Ralph Lauren Home, my beloved bust, which
is constantly on the move around the house, an
Indian stool, vintage rug and stack of books invite
you to sit and stay.
/
Opposite: Playing with proportion and scale
creates a moment in the hallway that always stops
me mid-flight. The ebonised Louis XVI-style
mahogany enfilade is the hero piece, layered with
monochromatic objects including black and white
books, an antique stone bust and a Trudon candle.
The photograph by Nick Leary hanging above, a
vintage washed-out kilim runner in similar tones
and an overscaled arrangement of oak branches
add to the striking overtures of the scene.

Even within the confines of a narrow hallway, you can create a mini story with just a few well-edited elements grouped within a soothing tonal theme.
/
Opposite: At Rosedale, the entry and hallway leading to three different rooms – the office, kitchen and dining room – provide me with enough space to style each zone individually but, through the use of a common colour and textural palette, they connect seamlessly.

214

Sometimes hallway spaces aren't long and narrow but divert from other spaces. By drawing the broader colours and materials of the main spaces into the styling of the console, this in-between space is the perfect conduit for connecting all the rooms.

Even though there are only a few objects on this vintage Italian console in this city apartment, they each talk to the space beyond, including architectural elements such as the black-painted door and architrave and simple honey-stained floor.
/
Opposite: A favourite phrase of mine is 'well edited'. This is about grouping together pieces in a vignette that either mirror or juxtapose with each other's shapes, forms and materials, so each one resonates individually and yet together they create a captivating whole.
/
Overleaf: Even without a surface or item of furniture to style, a hallway can still be defined with a few choice accessories, such as the intriguing antique Italian screen and overscaled terracotta pot with lush green *Colocasia* (elephant ear) plant seen here at Garden House in Sydney, designed by Arent&Pyke.

This bespoke shelving unit designed by
Arent&Pyke was overcrowded prior to styling.
As always when re-styling any area, I removed
every existing object so I could start with a clean
slate. I then slowly layered in vases, vessels and
found objects, using coffee table books to elevate
key hero pieces such as the large lump of quartz
and a vintage brass chapati box.
/
Opposite: Clustering objects to one side of this
cabinet created a focal point that contrasted with
the mesmerising weave of the pale Swedish birch
cabinet by Ringvide and the Jonathan Delafield
Cook *Poppy II* charcoal drawing on paper from
Olsen Gallery hanging above.

Repetition is a powerful tool within interior design, as demonstrated here in this open-plan living space designed by Arent&Pyke, where the stepped geometric pattern of the balustrade talks to the rounded silhouette of the armchair's back and base and the sway of the curved sofa.

/

Opposite: On the other side of the bespoke shelving unit (see page 220), objects are arranged in asymmetrical groupings, some set off-kilter to those above and below so that the eye is encouraged to move around the shelving, taking in every intricate detail. Meanwhile, the vase on the side table connects the two spaces by repeating the ribbing of the Guaxs vase on the shelving unit, but on a smaller scale.

This nook between two windows features the
first 'designer lamp', Oluce by Flos in brass, that
I ever owned, sitting on an ebony sideboard with
an Alana Wilson white ceramic bowl, alabaster
obelisk, a shagreen tray with pyrite, a Georg Jensen
bowl and marble sphere. This was my first foray
into creating a 'vignette' at home.
/
Opposite: A gallery of black and white
photography takes advantage of the wall's crisp
white canvas, but rather than floating it feels
grounded by the antique rush-seated chair
and wrought iron cocktail table below and
the richly stained hue of the doorway and wide
skirting board.

'*You can* CREATE MAGIC *in the* SMALLEST OF SPACES.'

This page and opposite: This unique wall-mounted console works proportionally within the narrow space, allowing for a simple styling moment with the branches of orange blossom mimicking the sway of the sculptural console, an oil burner by Henry Wilson and a trinket box in which to keep everyday items.

ARTISTIC MOMENTS I like to keep walls light and crisp and then add drama through light sconces or artwork – it helps to create a sense of height in a condensed space like a hallway, while providing a little snapshot of personality.

REINVENTING OLD FINDS Sometimes the shape or form of an antique piece can be right, but the finish feels dated, so I love to have pieces ebonised with layers of black polish. In Sydney, **Atelier Marmont** (ateliermarmont.com.au) are my go-to 'miracle workers' for repairing, polishing, painting or restoring any piece of furniture. They have helped me to bring new life to many pieces, including the dining room armoire, lounge room side tables and upstairs hallway cabinet at Rosedale. By 'blacking out' a piece, it takes on a new form where the detail remains but it instantly feels more striking and modern.

ANTIQUE & VINTAGE SOURCES
Graham Geddes Antiques, Armadale, Victoria (grahamgeddesantiques.com.au) for an elegant curation of antiquities and custom-designed reproductions from the 17th, 18th, 19th and early 20th century.
Galerie Half, Los Angeles (galeriehalf.com) for highly collectable mid-century furniture, lighting and accessories.
Miguel Meirelles Antiques, Malvern, Victoria (meirelles.com.au) for a mix of French fine antiques and rustic Provençal finds as well as architectural salvage for indoors and out.

SHELFIE EXPECTATIONS When I'm putting together objects on a set of shelves, I think beyond the usual concept of grouping things in threes. Instead, I might play with the idea of everything being tonal but sculptural, contrasted against a neutral wall. I find balance in placing the various objects asymmetrically: a ceramic letter with a vase is offset at a different angle to a small bowl; a large vase is placed as a singular piece on top of some books; something round and bobbly is set next to something tall and clean in line. I also like to overlap things – I call it cuddling – where some of the individual pieces could be standalone, but when coupled together they create more impact because the contrast helps you to notice the detail in each one better.

ANY SPACE CAN BECOME A MEANINGFUL MOMENT At Rosedale there is a landing where I placed a chair in a window space which looked graphically arresting but served no real purpose. I like to create spaces where you can sit and enjoy what is around you, and this landing is now one of my favourite places to sit because I feel connected to the view of the edifying landscape that sprawls before me outside.

Jamb London (jamb.co.uk) for a sought-after collection of antique and reproduction fireplaces, furniture and lighting inspired by the English country house aesthetic.
The Vault Sydney (thevaultsydney.com) for a mix of antique, vintage and modern design pieces.
1stDibs (1stdibs.com) for the world's best online resource for antique and contemporary furniture, lighting, objets d'art, jewellery, fashion and art.
Obselete Inc., Los Angeles (obsoleteinc.com) for an eclectic and sometimes kooky (but always cool) selection of antiques, vintage design and contemporary art.
Marché aux Puces de Saint-Ouen, Paris (pucesdeparissaintouen.com) for its labyrinthine sprawl of antique and second-hand dealers, including the lauded Paul Bert Serpette antiques market, a favourite with designers, decorators and gallerists (for a smaller open-air alternative, head to **Marché aux Puces de la Porte de Vanves** (pucesdevanves.com) for over 400 bric-à-brac traders every weekend).
Galerie Spadafora, Paris (galeriespadafora.com) for its speciality 18th-century Italian furniture.
Galerie LMG, Paris (galerielmg.com) for 'Le Magasin Général' curation of quirky and unusual mid-century furniture, lighting and decorative finds.
Ian Hadlow Interiors (antiquedecorativeart.com) for an always surprising mix of furniture, objets d'art, sculpture and fine art from all periods and styles.

All that this minimalist arched hallway needed was a bold cast bronze sculpture to sit peacefully within the transcendent beauty of the surrounding space. Design by Stafford Architecture.

IX

Entertain

The Garden

In the same way that we create layers and depth within living and dining rooms, so too can we achieve this with outdoor entertaining spaces. Thanks to the incredible array of outdoor fabrics now available, including velvets, bouclés and linens, and the trend for designing outside tables and chairs to look like indoor furniture, the garden really can be treated like an additional room of the home. I take the same approach to styling the exterior as I would the interiors, creating a natural flow from inside to outside that echoes the same style and spirit of the house. The garden can be so much more than patches of grass and paving.

The choices you make for outdoor areas should be very much dictated by how you like to live and want to use the space. So it could be as simple as a laid-back pair of curvaceous cane armchairs with comfy cushions on a terrace, or a series of long tables and benches because you entertain a lot. I like to be savvy about proportion – so not just having one great big piece of furniture or a set of chunky outdoor chairs, but perhaps a smaller sofa with an armchair and table to allow for an easier flow around the space if it is quite tight.

As well as considering your choice of tables, chairs, cushions and lanterns, have fun with your plant selections so that they reflect your personality. Around a fire pit at a house in Watson's Bay, overlooking Sydney Harbour, I dressed the built-in loungers with an abundant mix of geometric, ikat and embroidered cushions, teamed with lots of rustic textures, including scrubbed wood coffee tables, stools topped with woven raffia and tall bamboo hurricane lanterns, to give a welcoming vibe.

At Rosedale, a generous outdoor entertaining space was created in what had originally been the kitchen, with a great big fireplace at one end which had served as the oven. A fire had broken out at the house long before moving in and everything had burned down, so it was like a great big pit, overgrown with trees. In place of the old kitchen, a linear ornamental entertaining garden was created, lined with pear trees, to allow for three 3.5-metre-long tables that can fit up to 40 people. It is the perfect spot for having a whole bunch of family over or for throwing huge parties.

Setting the outdoor table doesn't mean using melamine plates, plastic cups and disposable cutlery. You can bring in anything you want. I draw on the look and feel of the surrounding environment for styling themes. I love to load big ceramic or metal bowls with whatever fruit is in season, lemons, apples or oranges, or dot terracotta pots of delicate wildflowers or fragrant herbs down the centre of the table. An assortment of vases filled with seasonal flowers works too. I'm very lucky to have a huge vegetable patch to source from – I like to use what is directly around me, so in the autumn that might mean styling the table with baby pumpkins and gourds, and in the summer, trails of jasmine, clematis or garden roses.

When entertaining outside, embrace the idea that it can feel a little more informal, but don't go so far down the relaxed rustic route that you forget to bring in a little glamour to elevate even the simplest setting when you're styling outside. Whether it is introducing metallic accents or bringing out the good crystal, fine linens and china, there should always be a hint of romance in your scene settings.

This page and opposite: Entertaining is my happiest pastime, which I luckily have the opportunity to engage in regularly at Rosedale, whether hosting family and friends for drinks or dinner, guests who attend my Masterclasses, or neighbours for Sunday lunches. There is no greater inspiration for me than nature, so whenever I create a tablescape or event in the garden, I draw on the surroundings for inspiration, but soften the space by adding decadent layers you wouldn't expect when entertaining outside.

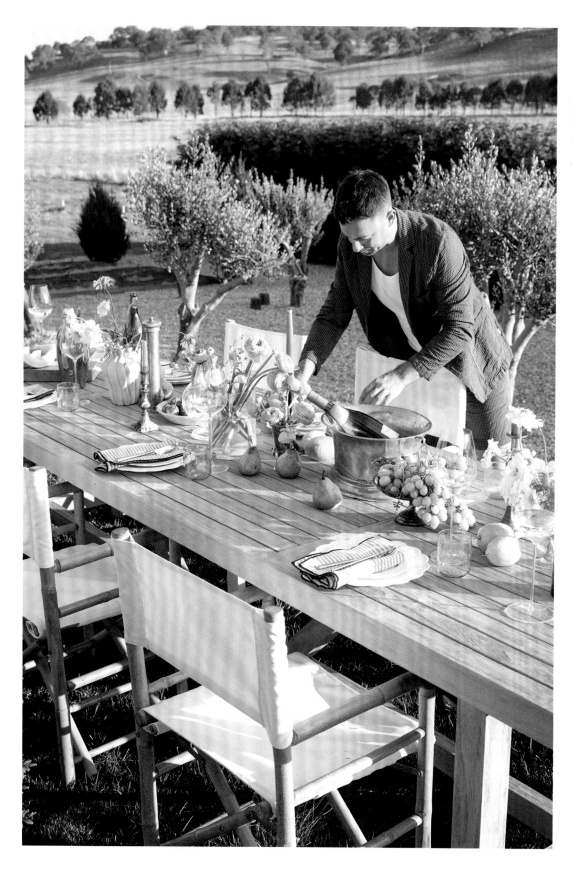

This page and opposite: I always start with a concept so that it can inform where I'll set out the table in the garden, what will be served on the menu, the colour palette of the linen, dinnerware and glassware, and even the soundtrack to suit the occasion. Given the Australian climate, I particularly love entertaining in the sprawling space where the original kitchen was once located, in the middle of one of the grassy fields surrounding the house, or by the pool.

238

While I am no garden expert, I admit to
creating a garden 'mood board' for Michael
prior to starting the renovation so that the
exterior informed the interior, and vice
versa. I wanted to be sure they both worked
together colourfully, texturally and stylistically.
This is one of my favourite times of day at
Rosedale, when the sun sets behind the house
and a gentle golden glow bathes the formal
front garden planted with foxgloves, lupins,
lavender and Japanese *Buxus* topiary.

This page and opposite: When styling with flowers, I tend to use a small variety of three or four different blooms in the same colour palette, grouped together en masse in multiple bouquets at different heights to create a sense of understated abundance.

'HAVE FUN *with your* PLANT SELECTIONS *so that they reflect your* PERSONALITY.'

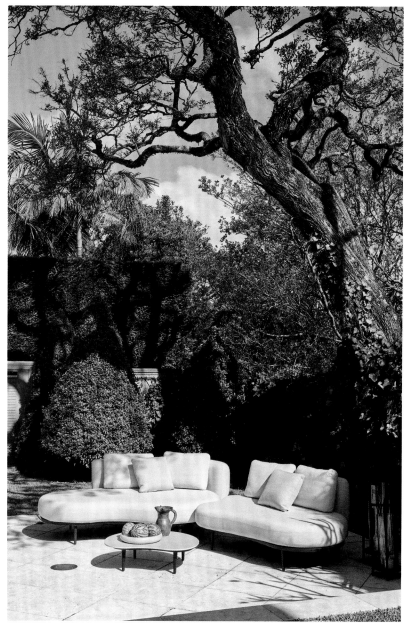

This page and opposite: In the same way that I would approach styling an interior, this formal garden, imagined by Parterre, also plays with clusters of shapes and forms at different heights, drawn together through a tonal palette of conifer, *Westringia* (Australian rosemary) and Japanese box, accented with sculptural stone spheres.

This page and opposite: Weather-resistant fabrics have come a long way since the days when outdoor furniture was upholstered in standard white, grey and black polyester. Adding a ticking stripe to this formal but still cosy outdoor space by Morgan Ferry Design gave it a chic twist. The graphic effect is softened by time-worn pots filled with balls of box, and violet has been allowed to grow up through the gaps in the stone flags surrounding the fireplace.

'*Don't go so far down the* RELAXED RUSTIC ROUTE *that you forget to bring in* A LITTLE GLAMOUR.'

It would have been easy to add plain cushions to this outdoor space, but layering a myriad of cushions fashioned from graphic ikat and Indian fabrics provides the perfect chilled vantage point for soaking up the unbeatable Sydney harbour views.

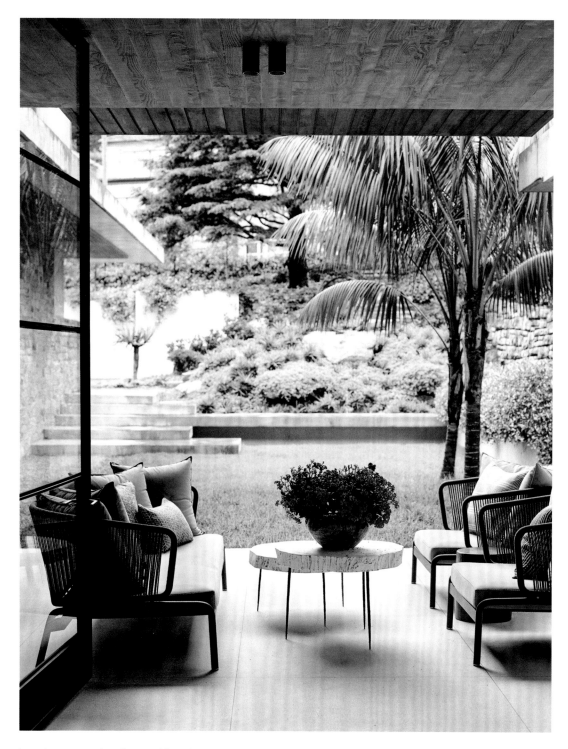

Lines between inside and out are blurred at
this house in Sydney's Taylor's Bay, with the
choice of Roda's corded tubular steel outdoor
furniture, which are modernist statements in
themselves. Design by Hugh-Jones Mackintosh.
/
Opposite: Even with a firepit in place of a
coffee table, the same styling rules apply to this
patio lounge room. Tactile materials including
timber, stone, concrete, linen and limestone
are layered, while keeping to a monochromatic
palette of geometric cushions and simple
foliage. Design by Hugh-Jones Mackintosh.

MOVEABLE FEASTS Think about the different ways in which you can create moments of joy as you move around the house and garden at different times of the day and year. Even if you don't have a huge garden, look at where the sun shines in the morning and put a chair there. With tablescaping, don't be afraid to bring the inside out to suit a particular occasion – lay out your favourite vintage cups, saucers and plates along with a freshly baked cake to create an inviting moment on the terrace for afternoon tea with friends, or bring out a table and chairs to sit under a favourite tree for a romantic tête-à-tête.

IN THE SHADE To combat the glare of the sun, a beautiful market umbrella or piece of linen hoisted up and attached to the house to create a canopy works well.

GARDEN VIGNETTES Rather than just placing all your pots on the ground, you can elevate them on top of a rustic bench, upturned pot or stone pedestal. In the middle of Rosedale's veggie garden I created what is almost like a foyer table, covered with all of our terracotta pots and accessories, as a focal point within the space.

THE BIG CHILL I love the duality of an outdoor space, where you can keep everything feeling clean and contemporary in terms of the furniture, but then transform it into an enticing gathering place with a big fire pit in the middle, creating a space where people can congregate with a drink, sharing stories and making memorable moments.

TOPIARY TRICKS Even a small outdoor terrace can feel like a haven away from the buzz of a busy city. In an apartment in Surry Hills, I created an enveloping moment of green by surrounding an outdoor dining table with a series of playfully trimmed topiary trees set in large, aged painted terracotta pots. It helped to transform the space into an extra room in a fun way.

BEST TIME OF DAY Dusk/sunset. For me it provides a moment to pause, to look back at the day, but more importantly, to focus positively on what is coming next.

FAVOURITE ESCAPES My heart is always with Italy in the summer, particularly Milan, Lake Como, Umbria and the Amalfi coast. New York City is the most vibrant, inspiring city that always shifts my design aesthetic. London and Paris for the galleries, antiques and design stores. India for the pure sensory overload and play of colour and texture. And Dubai and Istanbul for their vibrancy and culture.

DREAM PROJECT A 'renovator's dream' house in Italy that I could really sink my teeth into, especially if it means escaping to the European sunshine during the Australian winter.

WHAT IT MEANS TO BE AUSTRALIAN There is a laid-back and playful essence to being Australian, which is reflected in my design style, in the way I introduce personality into a space through nuanced stories and a general sense of ease. We are also lucky to have a culture that embraces the outdoors, so this verdant vibrancy and love of natural daylight flows through our homes too. Most of all, Australians aren't bound by the centuries-old decorating traditions of Asia and Europe, so we happily draw on a multitude of influences from around the world, mixing styles and eras in an upbeat, fresh and modern way.

Having a beautiful house with a wraparound verandah has always been one of my greatest dreams. The dining area set in this corner of the house at Rosedale, overlooking the horses in the paddock and the lush garden beyond, has become my very favourite moment at home.

Credits

Pages 32–33 and 103
Artwork by Felix Forest

Page 102
Artwork by James Gleeson

Page 109
Artwork by Nick Leary

Page 134
Artwork by Studio of the Sun

Page 189
Artwork by Michael Cusack

Images are copyright the following photographers. The page numbers designate where their work has been featured.

Anson Smart (ansonsmart.com): 17, 25, 48, 49, 54, 55, 60, 61, 68, 69, 87, 104–105, 112, 113, 128, 138, 139, 144, 158, 159, 180, 196, 197, 218-219, 226, 227, 229, 248, 249; **Edward Urrutia** (edward-urrutia. com): 21, 119, 238; **Felix Forest** (felixforest.com): 35, 45, 58, 63, 70-71, 72, 73, 88, 100, 101, 111, 115, 131, 160, 161, 164, 165, 175, 181, 185, 190, 191, 192, 193, 203, 217, 220, 221, 222, 225, 251; **Georgina Egan** (georginaegan.com): cover, 14,16, 18, 19, 23, 27, 32–33, 34, 36, 37, 40, 41, 42, 43, 46–47, 50, 51, 56, 57, 59, 74–75, 77, 78, 80, 81, 82–83, 84, 85, 89, 91, 96–97, 98, 99, 103, 106, 107, 108, 109, 114, 116–117, 124, 127, 129, 130, 132, 134, 135, 140, 141, 152, 153, 162, 163, 168, 169, 170, 171, 173, 183, 199, 208, 209, 210, 211, 212, 213, 223, 224, 234, 235, 236, 237, 240, 242, 243, 253; **Hugh Stewart** (hughstewart.com): 255 **Kristina Soljo** (@ksoljointeriors): 20, 126, 133, 147, 172, 194-195; **Monique Lovick** (moniquelovick.com): 15, 241; **Nick Watt** (nicholaswatt.com): 38–39, 79, 102, 110, 157, 246; **Prue Ruscoe** (prueruscoe.com): 15, 22, 44, 76, 86, 142-143, 145, 154-155, 156, 182, 184, 198, 200, 244, 245; **Tom Ferguson** (tomferguson.com.au): 24, 52–53, 125, 136-137, 166-167, 186-187, 188, 189, 201, 214, 216.

Acknowledgements

I could never have dreamed when I began my career as an assistant stylist 18 years ago that I would get to surround myself with so many incredible creatives who have not only become friends but family. Turning up to my very first photoshoot (overdressed) as an assistant and meeting Imogen Naylor (then interior design editor of *Belle*) not only made me realise I was on the right path, but I met one of my very best friends who has taught me more than I could ever thank her for. Thank you also to Neale Whitaker for making this chance happen, and for giving me my first break in the magical world of magazines.

Thanks go to my very dearest friend and media powerhouse Tanya Buchanan for not only guiding my career over almost two decades, but also for being my closest confidante and sounding board, helping shape who I am today. And also for the laughs. The many, many laughs.

Creativity is never an individual practice, and I have had the great fortune of working with incredible photographers over the years on editorial, advertising and social campaigns who have helped me develop my skills as a stylist and grow as a person. Edward Urrutia, Anson Smart, Felix Forest, Prue Ruscoe, Tom Ferguson, Nick Watt, Kristina Soljo and Monique Lovick – thank you for sharing your talent and wisdom, and for providing compelling images that tell the story of my world within these pages. Georgina Egan – not only do I always have the best time creating with you, but you make magic happen time and time again. Through your captivating images you have brought the stories in my very first book to life, for which I am beyond grateful.

Moving furniture from one room to the next, packing cars to the brim with vases, candles and cushions, and packing and unpacking boxes is half of my job and one that I could not, and would not want to, do alone. After 10 years of working together, Olga Lewis has seen it all – laughing, zjooshing and sending memes all the way along. I am beyond grateful for you and your style, and for being by my side on this journey. Also to Lucia Braham, Ainsley Sullivan, Alice Macmillan, Milli Grigg and Joanna Curran for being powerhouses in styling and management, steering this ship so seamlessly.

Getting to style homes for interior designers and architects that I have looked up to throughout my career is something that I will always be grateful for, along with the friendships I have made along the way. To my dear friends Juliette Arent and Sarah Jane Pyke of Arent&Pyke, Morgan Ferry of Morgan Ferry Design and Simple Studio, Justine Hugh-Jones of Hugh-Jones Mackintosh, Miriam Fanning of Mim Design, Alexander & Co., and Stafford Architects – thanks to you all for allowing me to sprinkle styling dust onto your beautiful projects.

To every store and brand that has built these styling stories with me over the years, as well as allowing me to make my dream home at Rosedale a possibility – I quite simply could not have done it without you. Thank you Cadrys 1952, Simple Studio, Porter's Paints, Dulux, Miele, MCM House, CDK Stone, Winchester Interiors, The Montauk Lighting Co., Boyac, Westbury, Anthony Kennedy, Tamsin Johnson, The Vault Sydney, Winnings, The English Tapware Company, Di Lorenzo Tiles and Phillip Jeffries – to name a few.

Thanks to my dearest friend Fiona McCarthy for so eloquently moulding my right-brain styling ramblings into poignant words that tell the stories that sum up not only my passion for styling, but also capture the heart of how to truly make a house a home, filled with joy and emotion.

To my editor Chelsea Edwards and the team at Hardie Grant UK, thank you for being with me every step of the way in producing my first book which encapsulates 18 years of creating and styling so perfectly. It has truly been a pleasure working with you.

My gratitude to Michael for the vision, knowledge and passion that he brought to the creation and evolution of Rosedale.

To my mum and dad… thanks for teaching me so much and demonstrating the importance of drive and hard work, but most of all for showing me what it means to create a home filled with warmth, support, kindness, laughter, deliciousness and joy. And thank you to my siblings Amanda, Victor, Adam and Helen (and my nieces and nephews Sara, Xavier, Jayson and Evangelina). You have all played an integral part in every happy moment this book represents… precious time with family and friends will always be my favourite moments at home.

About The Author

Steve Cordony is Australia's leading interior design personality and content collaborator, as well as a contributing editor for Australian magazines *Belle* and *WISH*. A lively, upbeat, and talented voice in the design sphere, Steve is a tastemaker who seamlessly matches his indisputable style and flair with an entrepreneurial spirit that he lends to his many standout projects, including Rosedale Farm and styling events held across Australia and, soon, worldwide. Here, Steve showcases his interior design and styling skills while opening his little black book of industry secrets to a special select audience. Steve lives between Sydney and Orange, NSW with English springer spaniels, Bedford and Wrenn.

Quadrille, Penguin Random House UK, One Embassy Gardens, 8 Viaduct Gardens, London SW11 7BW

Quadrille Publishing Limited is part of the Penguin Random House group of companies whose addresses can be found at global.penguinrandomhouse.com

Published by Quadrille in 2025

www.penguin.co.uk

A CIP catalogue record for this book is available from the British Library

ISBN: 9781784887421
10 9 8 7 6 5 4 3 2 1

Publishing Director: Kajal Mistry
Acting Editorial Director: Judith Hannam
Managing Editor: Chelsea Edwards
Internal Design: Studio Polka
Cover Design: Stuart Hardie
Copyeditor: Gaynor Sermon
Proofreader: Clare Double
Senior Production Controller: Gary Hayes

Colour reproduction by p2d
Printed in China by C&C Offset Printing Co., Ltd

The authorised representative in the EEA is Penguin Random House Ireland, Morrison Chambers, 32 Nassau Street, Dublin D02 YH68.

Penguin Random House is committed to a sustainable future for our business, our readers and our planet. This book is made from Forest Stewardship Council® certified paper.